# IMPACTING LIVES

## MY JOURNEY AS AN INTERNATIONAL DEVELOPMENT BANKER

## DR. KAISER NASEEM

INDIA • SINGAPORE • MALAYSIA

# Contents

# Acknowledgments

*First and foremost, I want to thank my family – my dear wife, Saira, who has stood by me through the last 41 years, patiently giving her unwavering support during my very frequent and hectic travels. And to my lovely children, Sahar, Hammad, Hisham, and Anusheh, who spent many days growing up without me being at home. I know you missed me during these long trips of mine, as much as I missed you.*

*I am grateful to my colleagues and mentors at IFC and all the other Institutions I have worked at. I learned a lot from all of you; of what to do and what not to do. Your guidance and encouragement have been key to my growth in the field of international development.*

*A big thank you to the teams I worked with in the many countries I travelled to. Without your support, the work I was doing would not have been possible. Your commitment and hard work made everything possible, and I couldn't have done it without you.*

*I also want to thank the team at Notion Press for their continuous support and for seeing the book through to publication.*

*Finally, I want to thank the readers, and everyone involved or interested in making this world a better place for all of us. I sincerely hope this book offers insights and encourages others to keep pushing for positive change.*

# Preface

Every new evolution starts with a single step, and for me, that step was taken over forty years ago when I began my journey in development finance. This book reflects that journey—a path that has taken me across different parts of the world and through various stages of life, from my early days in Pakistan to working with some of the world's most important financial institutions globally. Along the way, I've seen firsthand how international development efforts touch people's lives in different corners of the world.

So why am I writing this book now? The world is facing challenges more complex than ever before. From political instability and economic inequalities to environmental crises, developing nations are feeling the pressure. In times like these, I feel an urgent need to share the experiences and lessons I've gathered throughout my career in international development. Sustainable economic development is no longer a choice—it's a necessity.

This book is not just about my personal career; it's about the broader story of development finance and how it affects people's lives across the globe. Through this book, I want to offer a glimpse into how development work is carried out by international institutions like the World Bank Group and why these institutions, despite their best efforts, sometimes fall short of their potential. Is it their structure, politics, or something deeper that prevents them from making a larger impact? These are the questions I attempt to address based on my own observations and experiences.

As I speak about my journey, I highlight some key events that readers might recall, such as the Cold War era and its impact on the world at large, Pakistan's continuing economic roller coaster ride, and how young nations like Uzbekistan have today positioned themselves for growth. These are moments in history that have shaped the world of development finance and serve as lessons for professionals, students, and anyone interested in the field of international development.

I've had the privilege of witnessing the ups and downs of economic progress—from the optimism of the 1970s to the uncertainties of today. Through these pages, I aim to share insights on the role of development finance and the balance that needs to be struck between economic growth and social justice. I also touch on the lessons learned, the challenges overcome, and the milestones achieved through persistence and dedication.

In writing this book, my goal is to offer, in simple language, a personal perspective on a field that can often seem distant or complex. I want this book to be accessible to everyone—whether you're a development professional, an economic planner, a student, or simply curious about how development finance shapes everyday lives and builds nations. I aim to show how decisions made at the highest levels can impact millions, and how, even with the best intentions, results can sometimes miss the mark.

This is not just a reflection on the past; it's also a call to look forward. Now, more than ever, we need to learn from our past experiences and adapt to the rapid changes around us. I hope that this book will help practicing and aspiring development professionals, students, and anyone interested in these topics gain a clearer understanding of the importance of development work and the role it plays in improving lives.

In the chapters that follow, I'll share my experiences working with the world's largest development finance institution, the World Bank Group (WBG). Throughout these stories, you'll see the world I've been a part of for over four decades. I hope that by sharing this journey, I can inspire others to approach development work with the same passion and commitment that have guided me.

Thank you for picking up this book. As you read through these pages, I hope you gain a deeper understanding of the challenges in development finance and see the human side of it—where every decision, every policy, and every project has the potential to create real change in people's lives.

This isn't just my story. It's the story of the many people, communities, and countries I've had the privilege to work with. It's a story of perseverance, hard work, and a belief that with the right approach, we can create meaningful change in the world.

Chapter 1

# Early Years – 1971 to 1984

As I boarded the plane from Karachi to Moscow, the capital of the Union of Soviet Socialists Republics (USSR), in late August 1971, I couldn't help but reflect on how life had taken such an unexpected turn. Just a few months earlier, I had graduated from the Pakistan Air Force (PAF) Public School in Sargodha, Pakistan, to become a fighter pilot in the Pakistan Air Force. Flying had been a part of our curriculum since grade 10, and although I had earned a solo wing on a glider aircraft, I remember feeling uneasy every time I was up in the air. I even wrote to my father about my discomfort. He spoke with our principal, who reassured him by writing in my term report, "Kaiser's being the studious type does not mean he cannot be a fighter pilot. He is still too young to decide. In our assessment, he is first-class Air Force officer material."

Despite their confidence in me, my interest in flying never fully returned. When the time came for the medical fitness exam before entering the training academy, I was advised to undergo a minor nasal operation. I chose not to have the surgery, which meant I couldn't continue with my pilot training.

With my path to becoming a pilot closed, I found myself free to choose a new direction for my life. I began applying to universities in the USA, aiming to pursue higher education there. One day I came across a newspaper advertisement that changed everything. The Soviet Union had announced plans to build Pakistan's first steel mill and was offering scholarships to 15 Pakistani students to study metallurgical engineering in the USSR. The opportunity intrigued me, so I applied. Although the competition was fierce, I was selected together with fourteen other students.

And so, instead of heading to the USA, I found myself on a plane to Moscow, ready to spend the next seven years of my life in the USSR. It was a time known as the "Cold War" period, a time when the world was sharply divided between two superpowers: the USA and the USSR. As I settled into my seat on the plane, little did I know that these years in the Soviet Union would shape my future in ways I could never have imagined.

The USSR was a vast union of multiple socialist republics that existed from 1918 to 1991. It spanned much of Eastern Europe and Central Asia and was known for its centralized economy and single-party system led by the Communist Party. As a superpower, the USSR had a significant impact on global politics, economics, and culture. The period of intense rivalry between the USSR and the USA is often referred to as the "Cold War."

The term "Cold War" was first introduced by the English writer George Orwell in a 1945 essay titled "You and the Atomic Bomb." Later, in 1947, Bernard Baruch, an advisor to American presidents, remarked, "Let us not be deceived: we are today in the midst of a cold war."

The USA viewed the USSR as a major threat to its way of life and values. They consistently warned against the Soviet Union, suggesting that its leaders were planning to overthrow governments of other countries to disrupt the existing world order. As a result, the USA spearheaded efforts to isolate the USSR on the global stage. In response, the Soviet government informed its citizens that they were surrounded by hostile capitalist nations that opposed the idea of giving power to the people.

In March 1946, Sir Winston Churchill made a famous speech where he stated, "From Stettin in the Baltic to Trieste in the Adriatic, an iron curtain has descended across the continent." This "iron curtain" symbolized the division between the Eastern and Western Bloc countries in Europe. The Soviet government wanted to shield its citizens from any Western capitalist influences or interactions.

In the 1970s, the world was still divided into two major camps: the American-led Western Bloc and the Soviet-led Eastern Bloc. Pakistan had always sided with the American camp, so the USSR was largely unknown to most of us. Before our travel to the Soviet Union, we were briefed by Pakistan Steel officials who advised us to be cautious. They warned us to avoid criticizing the Soviet government and suggested that we might be under surveillance, with the possibility that our conversations could be recorded.

This made us uneasy as we arrived in Moscow after our 5-hour flight, and we found ourselves speaking in whispers, especially near places like air conditioning ducts where we thought listening devices might be hidden.

We spent the first two days in Moscow, carefully watching what we said and where we said it. We then boarded a midnight train to Leningrad, now known as St. Petersburg, where we would spend a year learning Russian. It didn't take long for us to realize that the warnings we had received were overstated. Instead of constant surveillance, we found ourselves engaging in open discussions with our teachers about communism and its effects on people's lives. These debates were often lively, and our teachers always responded with respect and thoughtful answers.

Leningrad quickly became a place I grew to love. It's a city rich in history and culture, with beautiful neoclassical and baroque buildings, canals, bridges, palaces, museums, and theatres. Founded in 1703 by Peter the Great, Leningrad was the capital of the Russian Empire for 200 years. Walking through its streets felt like exploring a vast, open-air museum, with every corner offering something new to discover.

Learning Russian in this environment was an unforgettable experience. At that time, few people in the USSR spoke any language other than Russian, so we were fully immersed in it. The language program was well-structured and effective. Beyond our classroom lessons, we were deeply involved in the cultural life of the city. We visited museums, attended ballets and operas, and made friends with locals. These activities helped us not only learn the language but also connect with the culture and people.

By the end of the year, we were well-prepared to attend advanced classes and lectures in Russian. The initial apprehension we had felt gradually faded as we grew more comfortable with the language and culture of a place that had once seemed so unfamiliar.

We moved to Moscow in mid-1972 to study at the Moscow Institute of Steel and Alloys (MISIS), a highly respected institution known for its rigorous academic standards. By this time, we were fluent in Russian, and all our classes were conducted in that language. Moscow itself was a grand and impressive city, filled with famous landmarks like St. Basil's Cathedral, the Kremlin, and the Bolshoi Theatre. While our studies kept us busy, we also made time to explore the city and build new friendships. With its excellent metro system, getting around Moscow was easy and convenient.

After completing four years of undergraduate studies and an additional two years of postgraduate work, I returned to Pakistan with an MS degree in Metallurgical Engineering in 1978. I was eager to begin my career with Pakistan Steel, which was intended to be the country's primary steel producer and a cornerstone of its industrial growth.

The enthusiasm I brought as a young professional was not matched by my employers. I quickly learned that in the workplace, politics, connections, and personal interests often took precedence over merit. On my first day, I was directed to a large hall filled with rows of desks and a constant buzz of people coming and going. I sat quietly in a corner, feeling out of place since I didn't know anyone. Most of the conversation around me revolved around the political situation in Pakistan, with the recurring question, "What's going to happen to the country tomorrow?" A question that, interestingly, is still asked today, in 2024.

In front of me sat a young man with a moustache, and a typewriter in front of him. After a few days of observing, I decided to introduce myself. I walked up to him and asked, "Hello! What's your name and what do you do here?" He replied, "My name is Shahjee and I'm a typist." I couldn't help but notice that I hadn't seen him type a single thing in the days I'd been there, so I asked, "But I've never seen you typing anything." He leaned in closer, signaling me to do the same, and whispered something in my ear that had stayed with me ever since: "No work, no mistake." It was a strange concept to me at the time, but it revealed a lot about the work mindset in that environment.

The next day, I decided to go back to my boss and ask for some real work. When I told him that I had been sitting idle in that hall for two weeks, his response was, "Are you Superman that two weeks of observation is enough for you to understand the work?" Despite his reluctance, he assigned me to the "Raw Material and Blast Furnace" plant, where I finally began working in my field. This experience taught me a great deal about people's attitudes toward work and how young professionals were reluctantly integrated into the workforce.

During my first year at Pakistan Steel, our chairman, Mr. H. N. Akhtar, was a friendly and dedicated leader. He was committed to making sure the steel mill ran smoothly. However, he had a habit of teasing those of us who had studied in the USSR. Whenever he saw us, he would make remarks like, "How are the 'brain-washed' engineers today?" or similar comments. When introducing us to others, he would say, "These are the engineers trained in the USSR. They've definitely been 'brain-washed.'"

One day, while I was in his office discussing work, I decided to address it. I told him, "You often say we've been brain-washed. But I believe it's actually the other way around. It's you and others who haven't been to the Soviet Union who've been influenced by Western propaganda." He looked surprised and asked me to explain.

I continued, "You often quote sources like BBC, Time magazine, or Reader's Digest when talking about world events or even things happening here in Pakistan. You accept what they say without questioning or checking the facts. That seems more like brainwashing to me."

After that conversation, Mr. Akhtar stopped teasing us. I think he understood my point.

During my four years at Pakistan Steel, I came to an important realization: most large companies around the world weren't run by engineers. Instead, they were led by people from accounting, management, or marketing backgrounds. This insight made me understand that if I wanted to advance in my career, I needed to learn more about management. So, I decided to pursue an MBA degree.

Since I was working for Pakistan Steel, I had to apply for study leave before I could seek admission to a business school. In mid-1982, I was allowed one year leave to pursue an MBA. As I was to get married in January 1983, I started my MBA program in June of that year, accompanied by my wife Saira. My classmates used to tease me that I was on a honeymoon at business school!

In 1983 there were only two institutions that offered a one-year MBA program to professionals with at least three years of work experience. One of them was the Cranfield Institute of Technology in the United Kingdom, and the other was the Asian Institute of Management (AIM) in the Philippines.

The Asian Institute of Management appealed to me more because it was focused on Asia, and most of the case studies were based on Asian businesses. At that time, I was planning to spend my entire career in Pakistan, given that it was a developing country with a huge potential for economic growth and in need of professionals like me.

AIM was established in 1968 by a group of prominent businessmen, educational institutions, and the Harvard Business School. It was the premiere management school for Asia at that time and still is.

I completed my MBA in May 1984. My wife completed a course in computer programming and later worked for NCR Corporation in Karachi, Pakistan.

Having both an engineering degree and an MBA was a big deal back then. Even before I completed my MBA, I got a job offer from Pakistan's top development finance institution called National Development Finance Corporation (NDFC). In July 1984, I resigned from Pakistan Steel and made the move from working in Pakistan's largest industrial unit to its largest development finance institution, marking the beginning of my journey as a development banker.

My wife, Saira, and I often talked about our ambitions and dreams. She used to tease me about the many years I spent studying in the USSR, saying, "You spent seven years studying for a job you don't even like and learned a language no one in the world speaks!"

We would laugh about it, but I always responded, "No education ever goes to waste. Every bit of knowledge proves to be useful at some point."

For example, my engineering degree made my MBA much more valuable. In my job as a project finance professional, I had to evaluate various projects, many of which were engineering related. My technical background gave me a huge advantage. I could understand the complexities of these projects, which helped me make better decisions.

In the mid-1980s Karachi was a vibrant and safe city. There were several newly opened cafes and restaurants catering to the young professionals who were just starting their careers. At lunchtime, these places were busy with people from nearby offices grabbing a quick lunch or snack and catching up with friends. My wife and I would frequently have "lunch-dates" since our offices were nearby. We would try out a different place every day, and would frequently bump into our friends, or make new ones. It's sad to see what has become of this city over the years. Like the rest of the country, it surely gives no hint that Pakistan has borrowed about USD130 billion over the years for its development. The money has certainly not been spent on developing the country's cities or on improving the lives of its citizens.

Having Saira by my side made everything better. She was always supportive and willing to listen to my stories about work and my career aspirations. Her perspective often helped me see things differently and appreciate the unique path I had taken.

How the Russian language helped me is a story for later, but for now, I can say that my diverse education and experiences have always given me an edge in my career.

Studying at the PAF Public School, Sargodha Pakistan (1969)

Briefing by Pakistan Steel officials before travelling to Moscow (1971)

The Group of Students travelling to the USSR with Pakistan Steel
Officials (1971)

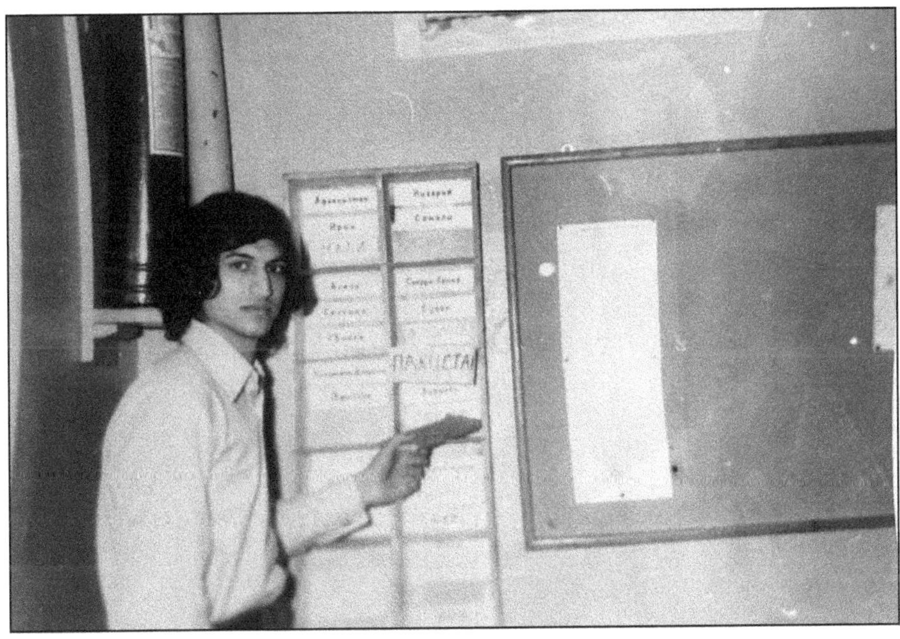

Learning Russian in the classroom (Leningrad 1971)

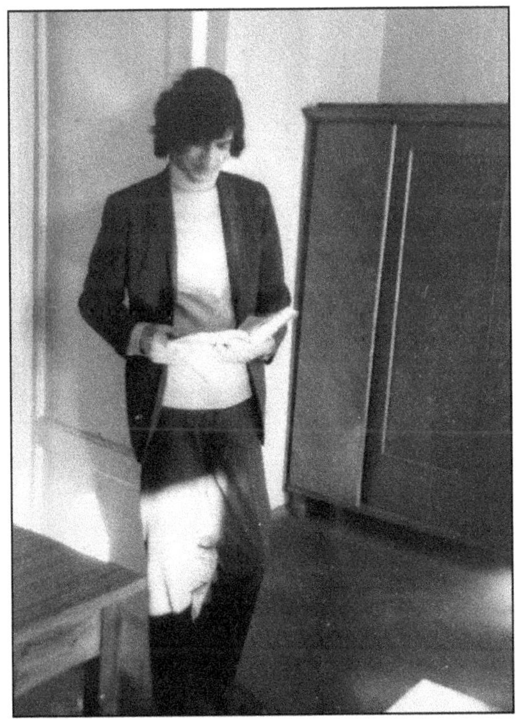

Reading a book in between classes (Leningrad 1971)

Learning Russian with my friend Khalid Aslam (Leningrad 1971)

At Pakistan Steel Mills with my team of engineers (Karachi 1981)

In front of the Asian Institute of Management (Manila 1983)

Chapter 2

# Pakistan's Economic Development - A Roller-Coaster Ride

---

Pakistan became an independent country in August 1947, after the partition of British India. From the start, Pakistan faced many challenges, with its population growing rapidly from around 30 million in 1947 to about 230 million today. The early years were tough due to a lack of resources and political instability, which slowed down economic progress.

However, things started to change in the 1960s. Pakistan's government introduced a series of five-year plans aimed at boosting the country's development. These plans focused on building infrastructure, developing industries, and improving the overall economy. Pakistan's progress during this time was so impressive that it became a model for other developing countries. The country was praised for its rapid growth, with an average economic growth rate of 6.8% during the 1960s. Even South Korea, which later became an economic powerhouse, took inspiration from Pakistan's second Five-Year Plan.

The growth continued into the 1970s and 1980s, with Pakistan achieving average growth rates of 4.8% and 6.5% during those decades.

But despite this progress, the country started facing difficulties due to various internal and external issues.

Between 1971 and 1974, under the leadership of Prime Minister Zulfiqar Ali Bhutto, Pakistan implemented a nationalization program through the "Nationalization and Economic Reforms Order (NERO)." The idea was to shift the economy towards socialism, a trend seen in many parts of the world at that time. The government took control of major industries, financial institutions, and public utilities. The goal was to promote public ownership and address the demands of workers for better conditions, which private owners often neglected.

Unfortunately, the nationalization policy didn't work as planned. The government faced significant challenges in managing the nationalized industries. Mismanagement and corruption became common, leading to financial losses. Pakistan's GDP growth rate fell to 2.84%, and the policy faced strong opposition both within the country and internationally. The loss of investor confidence had long-lasting negative effects on the economy.

By 1978, a new government decided to reverse the nationalization policy. They started a privatization program to return many of the nationalized industries to private ownership. The aim was to restore investor confidence and boost the economy, but the effects of nationalization were still felt for years to come.

Pakistan's economic journey has been full of ups and downs, with periods of great progress followed by setbacks. Despite these challenges, the resilience of the people has kept the hope of economic revival alive.

## Pakistan and the International Monetary Fund (IMF)

Pakistan's relationship with the International Monetary Fund (IMF) began shortly after its independence, largely due to the economic challenges it faced in those early years. The country had limited resources and struggled with low growth rates, which made it difficult to sustain its economy and meet the needs of its rapidly growing population.

In 1958, just 11 years after gaining independence, Pakistan turned to the IMF for financial assistance for the first time. The country borrowed $25,000, a relatively modest sum by today's standards, but significant at the time. This loan was crucial in helping Pakistan stabilize its economy, which was facing severe challenges due to inadequate infrastructure and the costs associated with establishing a new nation.

The need for financial support did not end there. In 1965, Pakistan once again approached the IMF, this time borrowing $37,500. This request came after a war with India, which had placed additional strain on the country's already fragile economy. The conflict had diverted resources away from development and towards defense, creating a budget deficit that the government could not manage on its own.

By 1968, Pakistan found itself in need of further financial support. The country requested and received a loan facility of $75,000 from the IMF. This period was marked by economic instability and political unrest, which further complicated Pakistan's efforts to build a stable and growing economy.

The most significant financial strain came after the devastating war in 1971, which led to the secession of East Pakistan and the creation of Bangladesh. The war had a profound impact on Pakistan's economy, leading to widespread destruction and displacement. To address the economic fallout from the war, Pakistan turned to the IMF once again, borrowing $84,000 to help rebuild its economy and stabilize its finances.

## Pakistan's Ongoing Reliance on the IMF

Since its early interactions with the IMF in the 1950s, Pakistan has very frequently turned to the organization for financial bailouts. As of end 2024, Pakistan has sought assistance from the IMF 25 times. The most recent request was made in mid-2023 when Pakistan asked for a 37-month Extended Fund Facility (EFF) of $7 billion, since the country was facing a huge economic crisis with GDP growth at only 2.4 percent, lower than the 2.6% growth in population. The budget deficit was huge, owing to poor tax collection, and revenues were about 12 percent of GDP with expenditures at 20 percent. The country's external account was strained with imports exceeding exports by almost US $27 billion. With significant external debt repayments looming, the country was at the brink of default.

Towards the end of 2023, a group of concerned Pakistani citizens wrote to the IMF's Managing Director, urging the organization to be more careful with its lending to the country. They asked the IMF to first make sure that the Government of Pakistan has the right policies, institutional structures and skills in place to make productive use of the funds before providing any financial assistance. Perhaps, owing to this concern, the IMF has become stricter, taking a much longer time to take a decision on Pakistan's request for a bailout. The $7 billion EFF was approved at the end of September 2024 and the first tranche of $1.1 billion was released a few days after.

The IMF provided the 25th bailout package with the usual conditions it has been imposing on previous bailouts. They want the Government of Pakistan to increase its tax collection revenues by about 40% through widening the tax base and bringing agriculture, retail and construction activities into the tax net. This is not an easy task and has been tried several times earlier too without any success. Nevertheless, the Government has given its usual commitment to do this, and as with other finance ministers before him, the current one also stated that "We are committed to structural reforms," and that the government would broaden the tax net, introduce reforms in the energy sector and implement privatization. He also stated that the IMF three-year bailout package was "a testimony of the government's "sound economic policies". The IMF has given similar testimonies 24 times before too.

Another condition of the IMF bailout was that Pakistan first raise $12 billion from other sources before IMF would approve its funding. This amount was raised from Saudi Arabia, United Arab Emirates and China. Together with the IMF funding, the country has now added another US $19 billion to its already huge debt burden. The country's economic planners have not yet realized that an IMF bailout is not an "economic strategy" but more of an "economic tragedy". The country has used these bailouts once every three years for the past 77 years without much to show for it. It remains to be seen how this 25th bailout money will be used. Meanwhile, the people of Pakistan continue to deal with the uncertainty that has become a part of their daily lives.

Today, Pakistan still owes about $14 billion to the IMF. Whenever the IMF approves a loan, it often encourages other lenders to provide funds to Pakistan as well. This has led to a growing external debt of about $140 billion. This debt is huge compared to Pakistan's total exports, which are less than $25 billion, and its annual expenses of about $60 billion. More than half of these expenses go towards paying off external debt.

This situation shows that Pakistan's economy continues to heavily rely on external borrowings, which includes the IMF and other lenders. Despite having reserves of natural resources and a large, talented population, Pakistan's economy has struggled due to years of poor leadership and economic planning. This has kept the country from becoming financially independent.

However, the blame doesn't just fall on Pakistan's leaders. International organizations like the IMF and the World Bank Group are also part of the problem. They have continued to lend money to Pakistan even though they know that the funds are not always used wisely. Instead of helping the economy grow, these loans often end up being mismanaged and misused. This raises important questions about how global financial institutions should target their financial assistance and continue to follow up with national governments on the proper use of this assistance to ensure that real impact is being made on the lives of the country's citizens.

## The Role of Development Finance Institutions in Pakistan's Development

Pakistan was still a developing country in the 1980s, with big plans for industrialization, which were driven by development finance institutions (DFIs). These DFIs provided both technical and financial help to projects in different sectors. They played a crucial role in setting up many industrial units in textiles, sugar, cement, and manufacturing. The National Development Finance Corporation (NDFC) was the largest DFI in the country and financed a lot of these projects, helping to build the backbone of Pakistan's industrial sector.

DFIs like NDFC got lines of credit from international development finance institutions (IFIs). These IFIs included the World Bank Group (WBG), which was the largest and most influential. The WBG provided funding and expertise to support development projects. They helped ensure that the financed projects were also technically sound and sustainable.

Working for a DFI like NDFC in Pakistan was a prestigious job. We were at the forefront of Pakistan's industrial growth, helping to shape the future of the country. My role involved evaluating and financing various projects, ensuring they were viable and beneficial for the economy.

Every local development banker dreamed of working for an IFI one day. It was seen as a significant achievement because IFIs operate on a global scale. They have access to vast resources and expertise, which allows them to make a substantial impact on development projects worldwide.

*For me, working with NDFC was a steppingstone towards that dream.*

In my office at NDFC (Karachi 1985)

Speaking at an NDFC workshop (Karachi 1989)

Chapter 3

# Working For the International Finance Corporation (IFC)

In the early 1990s, the Government of Pakistan (GOP) embarked on a series of reforms to deregulate the economy. They wanted to further encourage the private sector to participate in the country's growth. As such, GOP allowed the private sector to establish banks and other financial institutions. Since the nationalization of the banking sector in the 1970s, the service offered by banks to its clients had deteriorated much. Also, the banks suffered from government interference, especially in the granting of loans to businesses. The idea was that with more competition from private banks, the service quality would improve.

These were exciting times, full of new possibilities. Owing to my development banking experience with the country's largest financial institution, I was approached by a group of reputable private investors to help them set up an investment bank and a leasing company. This was a challenging role, which I readily took and successfully accomplished. Once the two institutions were established, I was appointed the CEO of the leasing company.

Back then leasing was a relatively new financing instrument in Pakistan, which had gained popularity with businesses, as it allowed more flexibility in managing a company's cash-flows. The demand for financing was increasing in the country, as more businesses emerged in the private sector. Many of these businesses had to purchase new machinery and equipment for their plants. As CEO, one of my main goals was to secure funding for our growing needs. For the local currency funding I was able to negotiate sufficient lines of credit from local banks. There was a growing need for foreign currency borrowings, as well, since much of the necessary machinery and equipment had to be imported. This led me to approach the International Finance Corporation (IFC), the private sector arm of the WBG to solicit foreign currency lines of credit for the leasing company.

IFC is the largest global financial institution that focuses on the private sector in developing economies. It had recently established a representative office in Pakistan. To seek assistance from them I needed to prepare a robust business case and information memorandum, which not only included the financial viability of the proposal but also showed that the company was managed by dedicated professionals. As CEO, my profile was included as part of the proposal. I took this proposal to the IFC office in Islamabad, which was headed by John Pott, a thorough professional who later became my boss and mentor.

John listened carefully to my proposal. He told me that he liked it and would forward it to the relevant people in Washington DC since the Islamabad office was just a representative office at that time. He asked me to check back after two weeks or so.

As I was getting up to leave, he unexpectedly remarked "You speak Russian." This took me off guard, but I confirmed that I did. He then told me that IFC was looking for development banking professionals who spoke Russian. He mentioned that I was the first and only person that he had come across with this skill. He explained that after the break-up of the USSR in 1991, 15 new countries appeared on the world's map and had become members of the WBG. The challenge was that no one in these countries spoke English, and no one in the WBG spoke Russian. So, it was very difficult for the WBG to work there. Furthermore, he said that no one even had any idea of the type of assistance these countries would require, as they had been cut off from the global economy for decades.

IFC's Islamabad office was delegated the task of engaging with the Central Asian countries, which were part of the Soviet Union and had just become independent. These countries were Uzbekistan, Kazakhstan, Kyrghystan, Tajikistan, and Turkmenistan. John thought that my knowledge of the Russian language and experience in development banking could make a significant contribution to these efforts. He offered me a job with IFC, which I promptly refused, as I was now the CEO of a leasing company and felt a strong commitment to my role. While John understood my hesitation, he asked me not to be hasty in deciding and to give the offer some more thought. He invited me to meet him for dinner after two days to discuss the opportunity further.

While driving back from the IFC office I thought deeply about the job offer. Joining the WBG had always been my ambition, and now this opportunity was being offered to me on a silver platter. That evening, I discussed the offer with both my mother and my wife. They both advised me not to refuse outright and to carefully consider this opportunity.

When I met John for dinner, the first question he asked me was, "What are you the CEO of?" and "How large is the company you head?" I replied that it was a US $5 million leasing company to which he smiled and said, "With IFC you would be dealing with billions of dollars in investments. And with just 5 years of IFC experience under your belt you can walk into any financial Institution in Pakistan." His words made me realize the magnitude of the opportunity. However, I also realized that I had a commitment with my shareholders to grow the leasing company, and even plan a public listing over the next year or two. So, while I had been convinced by John to accept his offer, I requested him to give me a few more days to speak with my shareholders. He understood my concern and told me to get back to him as soon as I could.

I spoke with the shareholders the same day. Fortunately, they were very understanding and encouraged me to join such a prestigious and well-known international institution. What they said to me was also very heartening to hear. The told me "When you come back to work with us after your stint with the IFC, you would be a much more accomplished professional. This would add even more value to our company". So, with these words I offered my resignation but promised to help them find a suitable replacement at the soonest. We were fortunate to have found and appoint a new CEO within the next week. I then went back to John ready to accept his offer. Looking back, it was the right decision. It opened the door for me to dive deeper into the world of development finance.

And so, a language that "no one in the world spoke" became my ticket to my dream job, which I started on October 10, 1992. Just two days later, on October 12, I was on a flight to Tashkent, the capital of Uzbekistan with a high-level IFC delegation comprising 10 senior people. They were all relying on me to bridge the language and cultural barriers we expected to encounter.

Sitting on that plane, I felt a mix of excitement and nervousness. This was my first big assignment with IFC, and I felt like everything I had worked for was leading up to this moment. The delegation members were experienced and knowledgeable professionals, and here I was amidst them, the newest member, bringing my unique skill set to the table.

My international development banking journey had begun!

Chapter 4

# The Significance of Development Finance

The international development profession is a fascinating one. It requires a lot of patience and a genuine passion to assist underdeveloped countries in their economic, social, and political growth. This happens by helping countries to better and more strategically plan inclusive economic development through good governance practices and responsible investments. When done right, it leads to better education, more job opportunities, and improved living conditions for people.

Development finance is used to fund and support various projects in developing countries. The goal of development finance is to reduce poverty and improve people's lives by boosting and sustaining economic growth. Institutions like the WBG, including IFC, play a big role here. They offer loans, grants, equity, and technical assistance to ensure successful projects that impact sustainable economic development and growth over the long-term.

Development finance takes a holistic view of economic growth. It supports and ensures that the necessary legal and regulatory frameworks are also in place to create a conducive and encouraging environment for investments by both the private and public sectors. It also ensures that the basic infrastructure, institutions, and networks are in place for inclusive and sustainable growth. This is very important, as everyone should benefit from a growing economy. This means creating opportunities for women, individuals with low income, and other vulnerable groups. It also means using and deploying resources responsibly and ethically.

Ensuring sustainable economic development requires that a country have well-governed government structures and institutions, as well as an active private sector that invests in adding value to the economy. This is achieved through establishing projects that can provide job opportunities for people to earn their livelihoods. Development finance plays an important role in all of this, as it enables both governments and the private sector to establish such projects, which would not be possible without such funding being made available.

Development finance also makes sure that viable projects are not only set up but are also able to achieve the purpose and impact for which they are established. The terms and conditions of development financing are usually more favorable in both tenure and pricing. This is important, as many projects have long implementation timelines before coming to fruition. This is especially true for long-term projects like infrastructure, power, and roads, which take a long time to complete.

A large portion of development finance is aimed at the private sector to promote entrepreneurship and the development of small and medium enterprises. Development finance is usually smart finance and makes sure that the borrower has the ability and capacity to use the funding responsibly and productively. For this reason, it is often accompanied by technical assistance (TA) and capacity-building advisory services, aimed at enhancing the entrepreneurs' ability to manage, operate and grow their business.

In keeping with the times, development finance today also targets climate change mitigation and adaptation efforts. Developing nations contribute less than 20 percent of global carbon emissions, and yet face the negative impact of climate change in the shape of increasing natural disasters, such as floods, drought, food insecurity and pollution. All this impacts the country's economic growth, poverty reduction, and human development efforts. According to the WBG, climate change could render anywhere between 32 and 132 million people in extreme poverty by 2030. For such countries adaptation and resilience are top priorities, which are being addressed by development finance. At the COP28 held in the UAE in 2023, the WBG pledged to increase the adaptation finance share of their total climate-related funding. This includes financing renewable energy projects, promoting sustainable land use practices, and enhancing resilience to climate-related risks.

By supporting these initiatives, development finance is helping to create a more sustainable and resilient future for all.

Development finance is typically provided by local, regional, and global development finance institutions (DFIs), of which the World Bank Group (WBG) is the largest provider to both governments and the private sector, the private sector being served by the IFC. These institutions are often referred to as multilateral institutions.

In addition to multilateral institutions, there are also bilateral institutions. These are established by developed countries to support other developing countries. Examples of these are the United Kingdom's Department for International Development (DFID), Switzerland's SECO, Sweden's SIDA, and Netherlands' FMO among others. These institutions provide financial assistance, technical assistance, and expertise to help developing countries achieve their development goals.

Development finance also acts as a catalyst to attract funding from other private institutions, which are more comfortable to invest alongside such DFIs.

The goal of development finance is to enable inclusive and sustainable development, enhance living standards, and alleviate poverty in developing nations. Through offering crucial funding and assistance, development finance institutions help countries in building the essential infrastructure such as utilities, roads, transportation and sanitation, and other institutions necessary for sustainable economic development and growth.

Chapter 5

# The World Bank Group (WBG)

Established in 1944 to help rebuild war-torn Europe after World War II, the International Bank for Reconstruction and Development (IBRD), commonly known as the World Bank, is one of the two Breton Woods Institutions. The other one is the International Monetary Fund (IMF).

The primary original mission of IBRD was to provide financial and technical assistance for the reconstruction of Europe after World War 2. It offered loans and grants to rebuild infrastructure, support industries, and help economies recover.

The World Bank gradually also took upon itself the role of providing development assistance to its member countries in Asia, Africa, and Latin America once its job in Europe was completed in 1951. These countries needed help in fighting poverty and building infrastructure. Over the years new institutions were added to the World Bank to address these issues.

Today the World Bank is known as the World Bank Group (WBG) and comprises five institutions:

- **International Bank for Reconstruction and Development (IBRD),** which advises countries in limiting poverty and enabling sustainable development by providing financing and economic policy advice to middle- and low-income countries.

- **International Finance Corporation (IFC):** Established in 1956 to promote private sector investment in developing countries. This is done by leveraging private capital and expertise to address development challenges, improve social and environmental standards, and promote responsible business practices. Today IFC is the single largest development finance provider to the private sector globally with a loan portfolio of about US $40 billion at the close of 2023.

- **International Development Agency (IDA):** Established in 1960 to assist the world's poorest countries. It aims to reduce poverty by providing zero to low-interest loans and grants for programs that boost economic growth, reduce inequalities, and improve people's living conditions.

- **International Centre for Settlement of Investment Disputes (ICSID):** Established in 1966 to facilitate conciliation and arbitration of investment disputes.

- **Multilateral Investment Guarantee Agency (MIGA):** Established in 1988 to promote cross-border investment in developing countries by providing guarantees (political risk insurance and credit enhancement) to investors and lenders.

Each institution within the WBG has its own role to play, but together they work to support economic development, reduce poverty, and improve living standards in developing countries. Their combined efforts ensure that projects are not only funded but are also successful and sustainable. Together with the WBG, IMF plays an important role in ensuring global economic and financial stability.

Chapter 6

# IFC's Role in Central Asia

I was feeling nervous as our aircraft touched down at the Tashkent International Airport, the gateway to Uzbekistan. The IFC delegation relied on my language skills to navigate our way through the consecutive meetings we had planned over the next 7 days. I had not spoken Russian in over 10 years and worried I might not be as fluent as I used to be. Officials from the Uzbekistan Central Bank greeted us on the tarmac. As soon as I shook hands with the first person, my Russian language returned instantly. I was still as fluent as ever.

If you learn a language in the country where it is spoken, you can pick it up very easily and quickly, especially when no one speaks your language, and you are forced to use it. Moreover, 7 years of studying in Russian had made it a second nature, not something easily forgotten. It was probably much like riding a bicycle.

The next two weeks were both interesting and surprising, especially for my colleagues. They found a country that had no idea about what the WBG was, how economies could be run based on market demands, how to price their products, or how to reach export markets. All these areas were previously controlled centrally from Moscow, the capital of the USSR.

Our trip aimed to understand what the country needed in terms of technical and financial assistance, and then develop a strategy together with the government. In late 1992, the important issues were privatising government-owned assets and providing support to citizens. Many people who were previously employed by the state suddenly found themselves without jobs and a paycheque for the first time in their lives. People improvised to make ends meet. It was sad to see museum guardians selling artifacts and paintings at throw-away prices to foreigners eager to get a bargain. Housewives sold household items like utensils and even light bulbs on the streets just to earn enough to feed their families.

It was amidst such a chaotic environment that we had our meetings with government officials from the State Privatization Commission, The Central Bank, The Ministry of Finance, The President's office, and others. It was very difficult for the IFC team to have meaningful discussions with these officials, mainly because of the language barrier and because of the terminology we used. For instance, when our director took about 10 minutes to explain what IFC was, why we were there, and how we could assist the country, it took me about 30 minutes to translate that into Russian. My boss was surprised by how long I took. I had to explain that while translating his short speech, I also had to explain what terms like assets, equity, and loans meant, as the officials were not familiar with most of these words.

On this trip, we also visited Kazakhstan, which was facing challenges like those of Uzbekistan. Together these countries make up around 70% of Central Asia's population. At the end of the visit, the IFC team concluded that privatization, promoting entrepreneurship, and establishing a robust financial sector were top priorities for these economies. Establishing a commercial bank was crucial because any entrepreneurial activity needed funding. So, our first project in both Uzbekistan and Kazakhstan was to set up a commercial bank. These were to be my first projects in my long career with IFC. We also recommended setting up a leasing company in Uzbekistan.

The way IFC operates is by first identifying a strong local partner. Local knowledge and connections are essential for the success of any project. IFC then seeks to involve an international strategic partner to invest in a joint venture with the local entity alongside IFC and provide technical expertise and training.

While searching for an international partner bank, IFC contacted a few of the global banks that we knew well. The first two we discussed the project with said that they had no idea of these new countries and were not willing to take the risk of investing there.

The third contact we made was with ABN-AMRO Bank in Amsterdam. We were directed to speak with one of their senior directors, Theo Bark. He was immediately interested in exploring the opportunity, although he too had never heard of these newly independent countries. But Theo, as we later discovered, was a risk-taker and someone ready to explore new ventures. He asked how to take this forward. I told him to hop onto a plane and meet us in Alma Ata, the then capital of Kazakhstan.

We spent a week in Alma Ata, where we met with different companies who had already set up offices there, like Chevron, PWC, Baker and McKenzie, and others. We also met with the local government officials, including the Central Bank. On the third day, Theo had already made up his mind and told us, "This country has a lot of potential. I can sense it and want ABN- AMRO to be present here when the country takes off". With his foresight, he could already sense the potential.

Theo then asked for a few days to discuss the idea with his senior management back in Amsterdam.

A week later he called to say that his management was excited, but there was a slight problem. He was ABN-AMRO's director for

Europe, whereas Kazakhstan was a country in Asia. In the same breath, he added, "I am going to tell management that this country is part of the former Soviet Union and it's in Europe. No one would be the wiser". And that's what he did. His foresight, gut feeling, and risk-taking enabled ABN- AMRO to reap the benefits of being the first player in Kazakhstan and later in Uzbekistan.

For the leasing company, we managed to bring in MayBank of Malaysia to invest alongside IFC in Central Asia's first leasing company based in Uzbekistan. The CEO of the leasing company, a subsidiary of Maybank, was an interesting person. While negotiating the terms of IFC's investment with lawyers of both parties present, the discussion at times would become heated and tense. At this point, the CEO would pull out his harmonica from his back pocket and start playing a tune. This would lighten the atmosphere again, and after a few minutes of listening to the tune, the discussions would continue. He did this throughout the three days of negotiations at the end of which an agreement was reached with which all parties were happy.

I was part of an IFC team led by Vijay Advani, who quickly taught me the ropes of how to work within the IFC and structure and launch these projects. I often referred to him as my "guru", as he eased me into the world of international development. For me, it was interesting learning and my experience of establishing two financial institutions in Pakistan proved to be very useful.

Within the next three years, both banks and the leasing company were up and running. These institutions were managed and operated by an international partner. Being the first such institutions in the country, they had a captive market and were able to become profitable in the very first year of operations.

Over the years these institutions trained and produced a cadre of young bankers who went on to work in newly established commercial banks and other international organisations. These institutions also acted as catalysts, attracting other similar institutions, such as Citibank, HSBC, and others to establish themselves in these countries. This was part of IFC's role too – to set up the first institutions in a country, and then draw other investors to those regions.

Simultaneous to establishing the banks, IFC also worked with the government of the country to design and implement a regulatory and legal framework for operating commercial banks and leasing companies. No such regulatory framework existed and had to be put in place.

Within the industrial and manufacturing sectors, the units were very large and needed huge investments to be taken over by the private sector. The local entrepreneurs did not have that kind of financing available to them. Hence, these units were broken into smaller units, which local investors were then able to buy and operate. For example, in the tractor factory, the foundry was sold as a separate unit. Similarly, the fabrication section, the forging section, and others were each sold as separate stand-alone units. In a textile mill, the spinning unit and the weaving unit were sold separately to new private entrepreneurs. Such smaller businesses required investments of around 1 to 5 million US dollars to renovate and modernize.

The issue with this model was that IFC's policy did not allow it to work with projects that required financing of less than about US $30 million. So, getting involved with projects that needed smaller amounts was not something IFC was used to, or even had the expertise to do. Nonetheless, as IFC had to assist these newly independent countries that were now members of the institution, a funding program called "Extended Reach" was set up, essentially to reach out to smaller projects in these countries.

I had the honor of spearheading this program, and we soon had a pipeline of small projects seeking IFC financial assistance. I quickly understood that the local entrepreneurs did not just need financial assistance but also required substantial technical assistance and handholding, which IFC did not provide in those days. I then reached out to IFC management to try and put together a technical assistance program so that we could make sure that not only was our financing properly structured but was also used in a productive manner to have the necessary impact.

Unfortunately, IFC management was not open to such an idea back then, saying that it was not something that an IFI does, although I believed that such assistance mitigates the risk of our investments. In any case, I sought technical assistance from other institutions such as the International Executive Services Corp (IESCO) of USAID, and the Canadian Executive Services Core (CESCO), which would send relevant experts without any charge. Such technical assistance was necessary before I could disburse funds, as without that the financing would not be productive.

For example, ensuring that the sponsor purchased the right equipment for the brick manufacturing plant that we financed, or that the layout of the machinery in the shoe factory we were financing was optimal to ensure proper workflow, improve efficiency, and lower production costs. Similarly, technical assistance was used for seeking export markets for the granite manufacturing plant we funded. These interventions greatly improved the use of our funding and the profitability of the projects.

The other lesson we learned was that lending to small enterprises was very different from what IFC was used to. For example, for the 2 million USD loan and equity investments in the brick plant, IFC paid about 1 million USD in legal expenses. We soon realised that this was not the best model for IFC, and we then designed a program to provide wholesale funding to other financial institutions for them to lend to the SME sector. The issue with this was that these institutions lacked the skills to assess and manage the risks associated with lending to small businesses. This gap in capacity hindered their ability to effectively support the SME sector.

This then led IFC to realize that they need to build capacity and skills within these institutions for them to be able to reach out to the SME segment of the market, which till then had been completely neglected not only in Central Asia but in almost all countries of the world, although they comprise 80% to 90% of all businesses in any country. Hence IFC's advisory services program was born in the early 2000s, something I had argued for back in the mid-1990s. The program was designed to help these institutions better assess, address, and manage the risks involved in SME lending.

The advisory services program later grew to address wider issues impacting global economic development. These included corporate governance, microfinance, environmental degradation, climate change, digital transformation, and others. More about this later.

In my 26 years working with IFC, I have served in several countries and across many regions. However, Central Asia, and Uzbekistan in particular, is a great example of a country being developed and integrated into the world economy from scratch. Also, more than half of my time with IFC has been spent in this region.

All these years of working in Central Asia with IFC were not only a great learning experience for me in terms of my professional development but also a great source of satisfaction and pride in seeing how IFC's several engagements and interventions had an impact on the economic and social development of these countries and the region. From nations that had no idea about international trade, economics, and markets, to ones that were now integrated with the global market economy and engaged in both import and export operations. Being rich in natural resources, these countries were quick to build forex reserves which they could then leverage to borrow in international markets for their growth. Improved regulatory frameworks and incentive schemes designed with the help of WBG enabled these countries to attract foreign investors to various sectors, such as mining, manufacturing, oil and gas, and banking to name a few. Within a short period, the region's countries were growing at a fast pace because of the advice and financial support they received from the WBG and other IFIs.

As I write this book, Uzbekistan is preparing to celebrate its thirty-third year of independence. It now has a population of 37 million. The country has taken the lead in transforming the entire region into one of prosperity and stability. It has gone from being a closed nation to one that now welcomes the world and is one of the fastest-growing countries globally with an average annual GDP growth of more than 5% and forex reserves of about US $40 billion.

Having Chai with the IFC team at a traditional tea place (Alma Ata 1996)

Launch of IFC's Islamic Finance Report (Bishkek, Kyrghystan 2015)

Addressing a conference in Warsaw, Poland (2017)

Addressing a conference about Digital Transformation

Addressing the the World Business Angels Forum – WBAF
(Istanbul, 2016)

On an IFC Mission to Baghdad, Iraq (2012)

At the Gaston Gregor Museum in Angels,
France after a conference (2017)

With some participants at the conference in Angels, France (2017)

Chapter 7

# Lost in Translation

---

As the saying goes, "There are many slips between the cup and the lip". This perfectly captures the challenges I encountered in my career. Often, there is a significant gap between what is planned and how it is implemented. In international development work, this gap can arise for various reasons, but one of the most significant is the loss that occurs during communication because of the different geographies and cultures in which we work.

Knowing a language is not just about being able to speak or understand words. It's about truly knowing the people who speak that language. Language carries the essence of a culture, the way people think, and how they view the world. When you learn a language, you're not just memorizing vocabulary or grammar; you're gaining insight into the people who use that language every day.

Communicating effectively is challenging even when everyone speaks the same language. Nuances can be missed, meanings can be misinterpreted, and messages can be lost in translation. Imagine trying to execute a complex plan in a foreign language—like Russian for the WBG staff when we began working in Central Asia in the early 1990s. Adding to the challenge was that much of this communication had to happen through interpreters, which often led to unexpected consequences and hindered the successful execution of our plans.

One of the key lessons I learned during this time was that language is not just about words; it's about culture, context, and understanding the subtleties of how ideas are expressed. This is why I've always appreciated the slogan of HSBC: "Your local global bank." It's not just about being present in different countries; it's about truly understanding the local context, the culture, and the language. It's about recognizing that the same word can mean different things in different places, and those differences can significantly impact the success of a project.

There were several amusing incidents during those times working in Central Asia, especially because we had started using interpreters who were still getting the hang of English and the tricky art of simultaneous translation. One such moment happened when we were wrapping up one of our missions for the proposed leasing company in Uzbekistan. My colleague and mentor, Vijay Advani, was known for his love of using clichés. As he was concluding the discussions with our local counterparts, the National Bank of Uzbekistan (NBU), he threw in phrases like, "We are leaving you with a laundry list of things to do," and "Of course, we are not asking you to rearrange the furniture on the Titanic."

Since I knew Russian well, I noticed our interpreter struggling to make sense of these expressions and trying to convey them to the other party. The NBU officials would smile and nod, but it was clear they were just trying to be polite. Then, suddenly, there was a look of confusion on their faces. Vijay had just said, "At the end of the day, we need to see the leasing company up and running." He paused, looked at me, and asked what had happened.

The interpreter, doing her best, had translated Vijay's phrase to mean that the leasing company must be up and running by the end of that very day! This caused quite a bit of confusion, and it took some time to explain what was meant. Once the misunderstanding was cleared up, we all shared a good laugh. But it was a reminder of how easily things can get lost in translation.

Another incident stands out in my memory from those early days. My colleague was explaining to the owners of a pharmaceutical manufacturing operation in Kyrgyzstan what IFC does and how we could assist their company. The owners were listening closely as my colleague outlined how we could provide credit, participate in equity, and offer other investment products. He also mentioned that IFC could help create joint ventures, find international strategic partners, and do matchmaking.

As the conversation went on, I noticed the owners suddenly looked confused. It turned out that the interpreter, trying to keep up, had just told them that IFC also manufactures matchsticks!

The word "matchmaking," which in business means connecting companies with potential partners, was taken literally by the interpreter, leading to a completely different message than what was intended.

Fortunately, I was there during both incidents and could step in to correct the translation and get the conversation back on track. But it made me wonder—what if I hadn't been there? What if the entire conversation had relied solely on the interpreter's translation? Where would that have left us?

How important it is to keep working on improving communication across different cultures and languages. It's a challenge that continues to be important, even today.

It's not just about speaking the same language, but also about grasping the meaning behind the words. I was reminded of this again when one of my IFC colleagues found himself in a funny situation involving a mix-up with a hotel name.

He arrived in the capital city of a client country. After landing, he got into a cab, and the driver started chatting with him. The driver asked where he was staying, and my colleague mentioned the name of his hotel. The driver then said, "That's not a good hotel. Why don't you stay at the 'Four Seasons' instead?"

Surprised, my colleague thought he had missed out on knowing there was a Four Seasons hotel in the city, as it was one of his favorite hotels. He asked the driver to take him there instead.

When they arrived, the building was in poor condition, and the surrounding area didn't look very safe. As they pulled into the driveway, he noticed the sign on the hotel read "For Seasons." It turned out to be a run-down, 2-star hotel trying to attract guests by playing off the name.

Realising the mistake, my colleague quickly asked the driver to take him back to his original hotel. When he later told me the story, we had a good laugh. Out of curiosity, we even went to check out the place in the evening. My colleague was definitely relieved he didn't end up spending four nights at that run-down hotel!

## Chapter 8

# Secondment to the Government of Pakistan

In late 1999, the Government of Pakistan (GOP) put in place a new economic development strategy to revitalize the country's economy. At that time the country was facing multiple challenges, including high levels of poverty, unemployment, and underdevelopment, which all required urgent and comprehensive solutions.

To address these challenges, the GOP strategy focused on four areas, one of which was to develop Small and Medium Enterprises (SMEs). It was recognized that SMEs had the potential for greater economic impact by providing employment and livelihood opportunities to millions of people. The GOP was looking for professionals with global experience to lead each of these sectors.

Given my experience in development finance with IFC, especially working with the SME sector, I was head-hunted for leading the SME development strategy.

I initially hesitated, as I was familiar with the complexities and challenges of working for the government in a developing country. Like most professionals, I also had a strong desire to contribute to the development of the country of my birth by contributing with the knowledge and experience I had gained over the years.

So, after careful thought, I accepted the offer. The country's finance minister formally requested the WBG president to second me to the GOP. The request was approved, and I took up my new role in early 2000.

In these years, small businesses had just started getting the recognition they deserved from governments around the world, including Pakistan. Certainly, SMEs have always been around and have always comprised more than 80% of Pakistan's businesses, contribute 35% to its GDP and employ more than 60% of the non-farming labour force. Yet, as in other countries, small businesses are not given due attention, especially in the context of access to finance and other banking services.

Earlier, some efforts had been made by the GOP to provide business development services to SMEs through an institution called the Small and Medium Enterprise Development Authority (SMEDA). In the absence of a complete ecosystem and enabling environment, there was not much that such an institution could accomplish.

Even earlier, in the 1970s and 80s GOP had tried to address the financing needs of small businesses through two financial institutions called Small Business Finance Corporation (SBFC) and Regional Development Finance Corporation (RDFC). For various reasons, mainly government interference, both institutions were unable to accomplish much, although the SME segment has a huge potential because of its entrepreneurial capacity and its ability to earn foreign exchange for the country.

In the earlier part of the 21st century providing banking and finance services to SMEs was not something banks wanted to do. This was an era when project finance and corporate deals were at their peak and commercial banks were very happy to work with a few large and relatively less risky companies to meet their lending and profitability targets. Of course, any surplus liquidity could be lent to the GOP at very attractive rates, as they were always in need of funds to cover their expenses.

GOP had now decided to create a new bank exclusively targeting small businesses. The onus of doing this fell on my shoulders. I quickly found out that this new bank was going to be a restructuring of the two existing institutions, SBFC and RDFC. I recalled John Pott's words when he had said, "You can walk into any financial institution", and here I now was, the Chief Executive Officer of SBFC and RDFC, albeit with 90% non-performing loans amounting to approximately USD6 million.

The situation at both institutions was very challenging, to say the least. The institutions were poorly managed with fictitious borrowers, weak credit procedures, and hardly any follow-up for collections. On top of that, they were overstaffed, with employees who had been around for decades but produced very little in terms of results.

I accepted the challenge but very soon realized that "reforming" did not make sense and would not work. I identified pockets of good within both institutions and ring-fenced some performing assets, which were less than 5% of the portfolio. I then identified a few dedicated employees to build two core teams, one to manage the existing performing loans, and the other to recover overdue repayments.

Our recovery efforts paid off and we were able to collect more than 50% of the outstanding amount within one year. I was surprised that most of the recovery was not due to some brilliant "work-out" strategy but simply picking up the phone and asking for our loan to be repaid. On enquiring from the clients as to why they did not repay the loan when it had become due several years ago, the overwhelming response was "Because no one had ever asked us to repay." They added,

"As a matter of fact, we were told that it did not need to be repaid." Of course, in several other instances, we had to take recourse to collateral, which was mainly a guarantee from individuals. So, calling up these individuals also paid dividends, and the recovery amounts were enough to fuel the reorganization and new lending efforts. We did not need any funding from the scarce budgetary resources of the GOP.

I also realized that continuing with the old names of SBFC and RDFC was not helping. These names associated us with the old way of doing things. So, we decided to rebrand and create a new institution where the assets and liabilities of SBFC and RDFC were transferred. By then we had two strong teams and provided them with both classroom and on-the-job training to continue recovery efforts and to develop a new credit portfolio.

We also developed new financing products that suited the needs and operating cycles of small businesses. The new bank was named "SME Bank" and our slogan was: "Where small business is Big business". We introduced SME Bank with a new image, new products, and most importantly, a fresh attitude and work ethic.

My role also included finding strategic investors to take over and manage the new Bank, as we did not want it to remain in the state-owned sector. This was again challenging because the GOP, while keen on privatization, lacked the political will and determination to carry it out, although I had already lined up some investors. After three years, feeling frustrated that I could not see the entire transformation through, I decided to leave the Bank and return to IFC.

Since then, several attempts have been made to privatize SME Bank. But, as is often the case, timing is everything. By the late 2000s things had changed in the banking world. After the 2008 financial crisis, corporate deals and big projects dried up, leaving commercial banks with fewer opportunities. To fill the gap, they started looking at small businesses, a segment they had always ignored.

SME banking became popular not because banks suddenly cared more about small businesses, but because they needed to find new revenue streams. With assistance from IFC and other institutions, these banks established SME banking operations. They quickly saw that if done right this segment could be profitable and help them diversify risk.

As a result, by the end of the decade, the market for small business finance was growing. Many institutions were eager to provide loans and banking services to SMEs. This meant that SME Bank, a much smaller institution, struggled to find its place. The opportunity to make a big impact had passed, and by then SME Bank was no longer able to compete effectively.

Financially, SME Bank was in bad shape. By the end of the decade, most of its equity was wiped out, and any potential buyer would need to invest a lot of money just to meet the basic requirements of the regulator. As such, SME Bank continues to drift without a clear purpose waiting for the owners, the GOP, to either shut it down or come up with a new strategy to revive it.

Conducting an SME Bank Board of Directors meeting (Islamabad 2002)

At the opening of SME Bank Pakistan (Islamabad 2002)

Greeting the Finance and Commerce ministers at SME Bank opening (2002)

At an SME Banking conference with my wife Saira (New Delhi 2002)

Keynote Speaker at UN Corporate Governance Workshop (2003)

Chapter 9

# The World Bank Group – Struggling to Remain Relevant in a Changing World

It took the World Bank less than a decade to shift its focus from reconstructing Europe to providing policy and financial assistance to developing countries in 1951. This change marked a significant transformation, as the institution expanded its mission to address the complex challenges faced by nations outside Europe. The World Bank has had to reinvent itself several times since then to remain relevant and continue supporting the development needs of countries around the world.

Since 1944, other International Development Institutions have emerged, each focusing on specific regions or sectors. African Development Bank (AfDB) was founded in 1964, followed by the Asian Development Bank (ADB) in 1966, the Islamic Development Bank (IsDB) in 1974 and the European Bank for Reconstruction and Development (EBRD) in 1991. These institutions were created to address the unique needs of different regions and sectors, providing targeted support that the World Bank alone could not cover.

In recent years, new institutions like the BRICS Bank and the Asian Infrastructure Investment Bank (AIIB) have been established. Today, more than 20 such entities are operating globally. They often find themselves competing to fulfill their mandates, but all share the common goal of promoting inclusive and sustainable development, improving living standards, and reducing poverty.

To remain relevant, many development institutions have had to shift their focus and expand their work into new areas. Initially, these institutions were focused on rebuilding Europe after World War II, and on helping the former Soviet Union transition to market economies in 1991. Today, these institutions are involved in a wide range of issues, including poverty alleviation, support for small and medium enterprises (SMEs), good governance, digital transformation, and climate change.

As these institutions adapt, many have started to operate more like commercial entities to compete with commercial lenders. This shift means they often work with well-established clients, especially in the private sector. But this approach has its drawbacks. Competing with commercial lenders not only displaces commercial funding but also ends up providing funds to companies that could have accessed loans from other sources. When this happens, the same companies may receive more money than they need or can use it effectively, leading to a waste of the limited development funds paid for by taxpayers of member countries.

Another concern is when these funds are provided to governments that misuse them. It's a well-known fact that not all development money is spent as intended. Some of it is diverted away from its original purpose by corrupt officials and politicians. Unfortunately, development institutions have found it difficult to prevent this from happening. Instead of addressing the problem, they sometimes end up giving more money to cover the gaps left by previous misuse, creating a cycle of debt. This debt is sometimes used by powerful member countries to exert influence over poorer nations. I'll delve more into this later.

Given its mission to "end extreme poverty and boost shared prosperity on a liveable planet," the World Bank Group (WBG) holds significant respect among developing nations. The influence of the WBG is evident in the fact that its staff can access the offices of Presidents, Prime Ministers, CEOs, and company boards worldwide. They engage in policy dialogues and provide advice on a wide range of challenges. This access and influence come largely from the WBG's position as one of the world's largest sources of funding and knowledge for both the public and private sectors.

From the 1950s through the 2020s, the WBG has been active in nearly all its 189 member countries, offering various forms of assistance. The results, however, have been mixed. While the institution has achieved significant successes, there have also been notable shortcomings.

In recent years, citizens in many of the recipient countries have begun to question the role of the WBG and how it engages with them. There is growing awareness of a gap between the WBG's narrative and the reality on the ground. Despite providing close to USD 350 billion to the developing world over the past several decades, many countries still find themselves struggling, burdened by debt, and without the progress they had hoped for. In some cases, these nations are in worse conditions than before, largely due to the debt they now carry.

Having worked with IFC, the private sector arm of the WBG, for more than half of my career of 42 years, I found the Institution to be an incredible learning ground. It is a place where one can gain exposure to all segments of the global economy and interact with high-profile government officials, corporate executives, and politicians within a relatively short period. The ability to work not only in a multi-cultural environment but also across continents adds a great deal of professional value.

When it comes to living up to its stated mission and vision, the WBG has often fallen short. For example, the primary goal of development finance provided by IFC is to assist private sector companies that struggle to access conventional sources of finance. These challenges might arise due to a lack of knowledge, a difficult economic and regulatory environment, a shortage of funding, or other similar obstacles. IFC's mandate is to support such companies and help them reach a point where they can access local and global financial markets for their future growth. Essentially, IFC should aim to work itself out of a job, meaning its success should be measured by how many companies it helps become self-sustaining.

Unfortunately, this has rarely happened. While there have been some success stories, like those in Korea and Barbados, these successes have often been due more to the efforts of the entrepreneurs and the governments in those countries rather than IFC alone. In many other cases, the expected impact of IFC's interventions has not fully materialized, leaving room for reflection on how the institution could better achieve its mission.

Today, IFC often finds itself competing with other sources of funding, offering better terms and helping companies deal with local regulations by using its influence as part of the World Bank Group. More frequently, IFC partners with well-established institutions in various sectors. The idea is to show success stories that others can follow, so they often choose projects that are more likely to succeed. This helps IFC stay active in the market, even if it means overshadowing other commercial financiers.

As the World Bank Group tries to keep its place in the ever-changing world of development, it takes on new issues affecting economic growth, though it tends to be a bit late in doing so. The WBG portrays itself as a leader in new ideas, but it serves more as a storehouse of knowledge rather than a pioneer. When new challenges come up, the institution tends to rely on consultants to provide advice to clients. However, these consultants are not always the best in their fields. Without enough supervision from the WBG, the services they provide can sometimes fall short of what's needed.

*Some of the issues that the WBG now champions, with mixed outcomes, include:*

**Fight Against Corruption:** The fight against corruption is one of the WBG's most prominent campaigns, and with its influence, one would expect the institution to make significant progress in this area. Yet, despite this, the WBG continues to fund governments with known corruption issues. These governments often need more loans just to pay off previous ones, leading to a cycle that doesn't solve the problem but instead prolongs it.

Internally, the WBG has struggled with maintaining strong oversight, particularly in monitoring the projects it funds. Oversight is often left to the governments receiving the funds or outsourced to other parties. For example, in Pakistan's education sector, the WBG provided substantial funding. Government auditors were supposed to visit schools annually to confirm they existed, with additional checks by independent third parties. For years, these auditors claimed schools were in operation when many of them didn't exist—later referred to as "ghost schools." These non-existent schools provided no education, yet salaries were still paid out to teachers.

There have also been issues in Pakistan's power sector. In the late 1990s, a WBG consultant was found to be involved in corrupt practices and was eventually removed. Despite these scandals, the WBG continues to fund projects where oversight is weak, which often leads to the misuse of funds.

**Good Corporate Governance Practices:** Another cause that the WBG has championed, especially since the Enron scandal in the early 2000s and the subsequent Sarbanes-Oxley Act, is the promotion of good corporate governance practices. In response, the WBG quickly brought in consultants to establish a corporate governance program, which was offered to clients to help them enhance their governance practices. However, during this time, the governance practices within the WBG itself were not always exemplary. The institution faced several scandals, including one involving the WBG's president at the time and his affair with a staff member.

I still remember the day this scandal broke out. It was the day before I was scheduled to give a talk on corporate governance to a group of top journalists in a client country. To my embarrassment, they interrupted my presentation to ask about the scandal within the very institution that preached good governance. I had to think on my feet and explain that the WBG had internal controls in place to address and resolve such issues. Fortunately, the President resigned a few weeks later, which helped to quiet the controversy.

One of the tools that IFC uses is to assess the corporate governance practices of potential and existing clients to ensure they have strong structures in place before funding is provided. However, this didn't sit well with many of the lending officers, who found it challenging to find clients with good governance practices in developing countries. There was pressure to relax this requirement, suggesting that clients should be allowed to improve their governance over time rather than having it in place from the start. Unfortunately, this approach didn't work as intended. Poor governance practices continued, even in institutions where IFC had a nominee on the board of directors. One example is a small private bank in Pakistan where the investment turned out to be a bad one, ultimately straining the relationship between IFC and a large regional bank that had invested in the Pakistani bank on IFC's recommendation.

**Ease of Doing Business Report:** In 2003 the WBG started publishing a report called the "Ease of Doing Business Report". This report ranked different countries in terms of how conducive their legal and regulatory environment was for setting up and conducting business. For these reports, 10 areas were studied and analyzed for each country, such as ease of entry, access to credit, resolution of disputes, availability of infrastructure, and so on. The WBG stopped publishing this report in 2019 owing to accusations that they were doctoring the statistics to favor China and improve its world ranking at a time when the Head of IFC was a Chinese national. Moreover, even the data collected from other countries was not always accurate, as it only captured the fact that the countries had the policies and regulations in place, but there was no follow-up on whether they were being implemented or not.

**Access to Finance (A2F) for Micro, Small, and Medium Enterprises:** In the early 2000s, micro, small, and medium enterprises (MSMEs) began to gain significant attention from governments and policymakers worldwide. During this period, government jobs were becoming less available as state resources were stretched, and there simply weren't enough positions to provide employment for everyone. As a result, there was a strong push to encourage entrepreneurship, with MSMEs being recognized as the backbone of many economies, making up 75% to 90% of all businesses in several countries.

Despite their importance, many of these small businesses faced challenges in accessing formal financing. Without adequate skills, knowledge, or financial records, they were often left to borrow from friends, family, or even loan sharks who charged high interest rates. Governments saw the need for these businesses to have better access to finance through formal banking and financial institutions, but most of these institutions were not equipped to assess the risks associated with lending to small businesses.

The World Bank Group stepped in to address this issue, drawing on its experience with the Extended Reach program in Central Asia. IFC began offering additional lines of credit to financial institutions worldwide, specifically for lending to small businesses. Simultaneously, advisory services were given to assist these institutions in developing the ability to evaluate risks and gain a clearer insight into the operations of small businesses.

To support these efforts, the WBG also collaborated with regulators to establish a comprehensive ecosystem that included legal and regulatory frameworks, as well as business support services. This enabled banks to better connect with MSMEs and dedicate a share of their loan portfolios to this important segment.

The initiative had varying degrees of success, and over time, the challenge remained in fully integrating MSME lending into the formal banking system. Many banks struggled to meet the required portfolio percentage for MSME lending, and the portfolios that were reported as such often didn't genuinely target these small businesses.

**Sustainable Development:** In 2015, the United Nations introduced the 17 Sustainable Development Goals (SDGs), a set of objectives aimed at addressing global challenges like poverty, inequality, and environmental sustainability by 2030. The WBG embraced these goals, as they aligned closely with its mission of "ending extreme poverty and boosting shared prosperity." Today, the WBG positions itself as a "thought leader" on how to adopt, implement, and track progress on the SDGs. Despite these efforts, as of 2024, the world remains significantly behind in achieving the SDGs by the 2030 target. There is a clear need for the WBG to intensify its efforts to ensure that countries are not only adopting these goals but are actively working towards and monitoring their progress over the next few years.

**Digital Transformation:** Starting around 2010, technology began to significantly impact the global financial sector. Numerous startups emerged, offering more efficient financial solutions to consumers and small businesses compared to traditional financial institutions. Initially, these conventional institutions underestimated the potential of these startups, believing that their long-standing history, size, and established client relationships would protect them from disruption. The WBG similarly observed from the sidelines until it became evident that these smaller platforms were starting to erode the customer base of large banks.

By the mid-2014, the WBG recognized the urgency of the situation and established its own program to assist the financial and other sectors in their digital transformation journey. Being somewhat late to the game, the WBG began to seek out experts in this area and onboarded numerous consultants to help educate clients and guide them through the process of adopting digital transformation initiatives.

Within IFC, there was a strong push to engage with client financial institutions in which it had investments, ensuring they understood the importance of leveraging technology and the risks they faced if they didn't. I was fortunate to lead this practice within the larger MENA region. Being based in Dubai at the time, I had access to a wealth of workshops, seminars, and conferences that were being held in the city. These events provided me with the opportunity to learn from subject matter experts and quickly get up to speed on digital transformation.

I soon realized that everyone, including the so-called experts, was in the same boat—learning about what digital transformation really meant and how best to adopt the new technologies. Before I knew it, I found myself on stage, considered one of the "thought leaders" on the subject. I must admit that my association with IFC lent a great deal of credibility to my words, whether deserved or not. I viewed this as an ongoing learning process; the questions from the audience often made me think about aspects of digital transformation that I hadn't previously considered. In many cases, the audience itself provided insights and answers, which enriched my understanding and helped me better educate myself.

IFC moved forward by partnering with several financial institutions, helping them on their digital transformation journeys, starting with designing digital strategies. However, IFC found itself competing with private advisory service providers, many of whom offered more programs to help companies adopt digital transformation.

Many banks still struggle with change, even though digital transformation is clearly needed. Some leaders are unsure about taking the next step. I saw this firsthand during a meeting with the Board of Directors of a large bank in Morocco. Their hesitation showed how holding on to old ways can slow down progress.

I was talking about why it was important for the bank to develop a digital strategy to stay competitive. As I spoke, I noticed some of the board members looking disinterested, staring at their smartphones instead of paying attention.

After a while, one of them spoke up and asked why the bank even needed to digitalise. He explained that the bank had been running the same way for decades, and in his opinion, it was doing just fine. He added that digitalisation was something for the younger generation to worry about, and they could take care of it once the current board retired.

I was surprised by his response. This was a clear example of resistance to change and the fear of trying something new. So, I asked the group who the oldest person in the room was. In 2017, that happened to be me. I then pointed out that if even at my age, I was talking about digital transformation, it showed that this wasn't something to be left for the future – it was something that needed to happen now for the bank to stay competitive.

I explained that if they didn't act soon, the bank might struggle to keep up in the market in just a few years. I also reassured them that technology wasn't something to be afraid of. Instead, it was a tool that needed to be accepted, in line with the changes and expectations of the bank's customers. I gave an example to drive the point home. I pointed out that while I was giving my presentation, many of them were using their smartphones—devices that rely heavily on technology, which they had adopted without a second thought. This showed that they were already tech-savvy in their everyday lives and had no real reason to fear technology.

This seemed to get them thinking and made them feel more at ease. The rest of the presentation went smoothly, and over the next few years, the bank successfully developed and implemented a digital strategy. This not only improved their processes and operations but also allowed them to stay competitive by meeting the evolving needs of their clients.

**Climate Change:** In the early 2020s, natural disasters like floods, earthquakes, and extreme temperatures became more frequent across the globe, affecting millions, particularly the poor. These events are largely the result of climate change, driven by modern industrial practices, the use of fossil fuels, and the reckless exploitation of natural resources, all of which have contributed to global warming. The World Bank Group (WBG) responded to this growing crisis by positioning itself as a leader in providing guidance and financial support to help countries and businesses prepare for what they described as a "low-carbon, resilient transition." The aim was to build economies that were green, resilient, and inclusive.

The WBG has been addressing climate-related issues since the 1980s and has today become the largest financier of climate-related projects in developing countries. Yet, the actual impact of these projects has been less than satisfactory to date. The financing provided has not significantly helped these countries in their fight against the mounting threat of climate change. One major reason for this is that the funding available is insufficient, and the financial and technical assistance provided has not been well-structured. Additionally, there has been a lack of a proper framework to assess the impact of these projects, which has further hindered their effectiveness.

As the WBG continues its efforts to remain relevant in global economic development, it seems to have lost its way. The need for development assistance—both technical and financial—is greater than ever. Although there has been some reduction in poverty levels over the past few decades, these gains are not evenly distributed and fall short of the targets set by the Sustainable Development Goals (SDGs). Most of the poverty reduction has been concentrated in countries like China and India, while regions such as Latin America and Africa have seen an increase in poverty levels. The gap between the rich and the poor continues to widen, creating significant disparities in living standards.

Global trade has been up and down because of COVID-19 and anti-globalization movements. These trends could have both positive and negative effects on developing countries, and they must be carefully managed.

By no means am I implying that the above causes should not be addressed by the WBG. As a matter of fact, they are all very relevant and the WBG has the clout to not only raise them but pursue its clients to also address them. The problem is that the institution does not use its leverage enough to make sure that the implementation of actions to address these issues is done in a more organised manner. It is as if the WBG is also just paying lip service to these issues by not properly delivering financial and technical assistance and making sure that institutional capacity within its clients exists to use such assistance.

Chapter 10

# Reforming the World Bank Group

The global economy has faced significant challenges, particularly with the growing debt burdens in many developing countries. This situation highlights a critical issue: the way development assistance has been structured, delivered, and monitored has not effectively achieved the goals of international development. From my experience working with the largest International Financial Institution (IFI) in the world, I have seen that these challenges stem from how these institutions are structured, how they operate, and the human resource issues they face.

In a 2005 speech, U.S. Treasury Secretary Robert Zoellick emphasized that the focus had often been on providing more capital rather than assessing whether that capital was genuinely needed or whether it was being used effectively. He pointed out that simply adding more funds is not a solution when the existing resources are not allocated properly. Zoellick also stressed the importance of ensuring that resources are directed to where they are most needed and where they can achieve sustainable and meaningful results. He further noted the U.S. interest in seeing development finance allocated to countries most in need, with the goal of helping these countries eventually transition away from relying on donor assistance.

One key measure of success for any development institution should be its ability to eventually render itself unnecessary. The true accomplishment would be to reach a point where there is no longer a need for such institutions because they have effectively fulfilled their mission. This idea was reinforced by the Treasury Secretary, who emphasized that development institutions shouldn't provide financing if the private sector is already capable of doing so. The primary role of these institutions is to support regions or projects that cannot attract investment from commercial sources.

They are meant to take the initial risks, helping to create markets that can later be sustained by commercial players. Unfortunately, this ideal outcome hasn't always materialized. Instead, development finance institutions often find themselves in competition with one another and with commercial lenders, rather than stepping back once a market has been established.

Back in 1951, when the World Bank Group shifted its focus to developing countries, it was practically the only organization of its kind. However, over the years, many new institutions have emerged, each focusing on specific regions or economic sectors. This expansion has introduced its own set of challenges. A significant issue has been the lack of coordination among these institutions. Often, they target the same projects in the same countries, leading to unproductive competition. This scenario allows client countries to negotiate for the best deal, sometimes even engaging with multiple institutions and taking on more funding than they need. Despite several efforts to coordinate the activities of these institutions, true cooperation has been difficult to achieve. Each institution has its own goals and must report to its own shareholders, making genuine collaboration a challenge.

The World Bank Group (WBG) is aware of the need for change within its organization. Even the then President of the

WBG, James Wolfensohn, acknowledged in 1995 that "the World Bank has got things wrong." He added that "every one of the things I've uncovered… has already been examined by my predecessors." Over the years, numerous efforts have been made to reform and restructure the institution. In my 26 years with the IFC, I witnessed at least six significant attempts to overhaul the system. Sadly, none of these efforts have truly succeeded. The WBG continues to operate as a massive global entity, yet its organizational structure remains cumbersome, with gaps in skills and delivery mechanisms.

What complicates matters further is the realization among the WBG's shareholders that the institution can be wielded as a tool of influence. For the shareholders, particularly the larger ones, the WBG represents an opportunity to reinforce their strategic interests and secure their economic agendas. This reality sometimes stands in contrast to the institution's original mission of fostering international development.

The influence of the United States within the WBG is especially pronounced. As the largest shareholder, the U.S. holds considerable sway over the institution, including the power to appoint the WBG's president. This position, by tradition, has always been filled by an American, leading to appointments that can be politically influenced. This intertwining of politics and development finance adds another layer of complexity to the WBG's operations, sometimes turning it into a tool for exerting soft power rather than purely focusing on development goals.

This delicate balance between international development objectives and the strategic interests of powerful shareholders is something that has shaped the trajectory of the WBG over the years, influencing its actions and the effectiveness of its interventions in the developing world.

It's clear that development finance institutions need to work more closely together. There's enough funding available to help build stronger markets in emerging economies, but the real challenge is making sure this money is used in the right places, in the right ways. If all these institutions share the same goals, then why aren't their strategies more aligned?

Maybe it's time for the World Bank Group to focus more on coordinating global efforts rather than trying to do everything itself. Instead of handling projects through its various regional departments, the WBG could let regional development banks like the IDB in Latin America or the AfDB in Africa take the lead. These organizations know their regions better and might be able to get better results.

Of course, this isn't a simple task, especially with the political issues that always seem to get in the way. But development finance should be above politics. By creating equal opportunities for economic growth around the world, many of these political problems could be solved over time.

It's time for these institutions to fully commit to their promises and start thinking creatively about how to make a real difference. The world is changing fast, and the way we approach development needs to change too. Perhaps the WBG could even return to its original mission: rebuilding countries that have been devastated by war. Sadly, there are still too many places in the world that need this kind of help.

The situation at WBG highlights a critical issue: while the institution is large and influential, it struggles internally with significant inefficiencies. The HR challenges and the shift in focus toward investment banking by IFC created a disconnect between the WBG's original mission and its actual practices. This disconnect became more evident with each restructuring attempt, none of which addressed the core issues.

Instead of aligning closely with development banking, the WBG, especially IFC, finds itself increasingly emulating commercial lenders, which was not its intended role. This misalignment has real consequences, not just for the institution but for the very countries it is meant to support. The focus on disbursement volumes over genuine development outcomes means that many of the WBG's initiatives fall short of making a real long-term impact.

In the background of all these internal challenges, there is also increasing pressure from shareholders, particularly from the USA. The influence of the largest shareholders often steers the WBG in directions that serve their strategic interests rather than the broader goals of international development. This adds another layer of complexity, making it even harder for the institution to stay true to its original mission.

Moving forward, it becomes clear that significant changes are needed, not just in the way the WBG operates but also in how it defines success. Without addressing these foundational issues, the WBG risks continuing down a path that diverges further from its core purpose of supporting sustainable development worldwide.

In 2019, in an effort to reduce costs, IFC introduced a voluntary early retirement scheme, offering substantial sums of money to senior staff who chose to leave. The plan was to replace these experienced professionals with younger, less expensive employees. As anticipated, many senior staff members accepted the offer, taking with them years of valuable experience and institutional knowledge. The new, junior staff who were brought in struggled to fill these gaps. Development banking requires a unique set of skills and deep understanding, and it quickly became evident that these new hires had a steep learning curve ahead of them.

The strategy was unsuccessful. Eventually, IFC found itself needing to bring in more experienced professionals once again, this time at higher salaries, effectively negating the cost-cutting initiative. It was another example of how well-intentioned reforms can sometimes miss the mark.

Despite various attempts at reform, the results have often fallen short. In 2022, German Development Minister Svenja Schulze, along with other World Bank Governors, renewed calls for the WBG to undertake meaningful reforms. The goal was to ensure that the institution could more effectively fulfill its mission of combating hunger, poverty, and inequality while addressing global challenges related to sustainable development. An "evolution roadmap" was drafted, and the WBG has since been working to implement these reforms, but the struggle continues.

Mr. Ajay Banga, the current President of the WBG stated in 2024 that, "under the umbrella of our Evolution Roadmap, we are working to become a better Bank. We will become more efficient and do more in less time". He went on to say, "We need to write a new playbook that will drive impactful development and lead to a better quality of life for people everywhere. Our approach must be inclusive of everyone, including women, young people, and others too often left behind. And it must be sustainable — through economic growth, human development, fiscal and debt management, food security, and access to clean air, water, and affordable energy".

"The World Bank will adjust its vision and strategy so that aid would be directed towards eradicating poverty and making the planet a better place to live" Mr. Ajay Banga further stated and added that the WBG "will focus on developing expertise and supporting all sectors that target the well-being, security and safety of humanity".

Despite all the challenges within the World Bank Group, it remains a place where those eager to learn can thrive. The World Bank's most significant strength is its ability to convene and bring together policymakers from around the world. I often think of the WBG more as a "platform" than an institution. This platform can be leveraged by its staff to deliver meaningful services to clients worldwide, but only if they know how to navigate its complex structure.

The bureaucracy that has grown over the years makes this difficult. Issues like inexperienced management, mismatched performance indicators, and short-sighted decisions can often hinder progress. But for those who focus on delivering impactful services, despite the hurdles, there is the potential to achieve meaningful results.

The strengths of the World Bank can be used for the greater good, but it requires determination and a clear understanding of how to work within the system. The positive impacts seen in different parts of the world are often thanks to individuals within the institution who have figured out how to make the most of what the World Bank has to offer.

These quotes from some of my managers provide a glimpse into the mindset of management and challenges within the organisation:

- *The evening before we were to travel to Tashkent on our first trip, our department director welcomed me to IFC. He also told me that IFC is a very democratic institution. Mid-week into our trip to Uzbekistan I expressed my opinion on a certain matter, which the director did not agree with. He called me that afternoon and said, "I told you we are democratic, but not 'that' democratic!!"*

- *"I know our processes are slow, but we need to push ahead with this."*

- *"Honestly, I'm not sure if we can work in this country, but let's proceed and figure it out later."*

- *"Nobody knows what the CEO is thinking."*

- *"I agree with you, but the Boss wants it done this way."*

- *"In HR meetings, leaders would say, 'You tell us what to do.'*

- *"I once told my manager that I could handle more work. After that, he stopped giving me any tasks. When I asked why, he said, 'You complained that I wasn't allocating work properly, so now I'm not giving you any.'"*

Chapter 11

# Life Lessons Learned Along the Journey

They say experience is the best teacher. And from what I've seen, it's your own experiences that truly matter—everything else is just advice. We only really learn once we've gone through something ourselves, and often, that learning comes in hindsight.

When we start out in life, we don't have much experience, just what our parents and teachers tell us based on theirs. But as kids, we tend to brush off their advice, thinking, "They're from a different time; what do they know?"

Life has its ways of guiding us, sometimes without us even noticing. It drops bits of information into our subconscious, things we can later relate to when we go through our own experiences. Over time, we build our own set of values and professional skills around these lessons. How we connect that knowledge to our daily experiences is up to us and plays a big part in how we grow as individuals.

Many of the values and professional principles I hold today were shaped by things I've read, seen, and heard throughout my early life and career. Over more than six decades, I've had many experiences, most of which have stayed with me, deeply influencing how I see life and what I believe in. Out of all these moments, there are five that really stand out to me, shaping my outlook and values, and they continue to guide me even now.

### The Importance of Treating Others Well

When I was a student in Moscow during the mid-1970s, I read a saying in a magazine, likely KOMSOMOL, that has stayed with me ever since: "Be nice to people you meet on your way up; you might meet them again on your way down." At the time, I didn't fully understand what it meant. But once I started my professional career, it became clear to me.

In my career, I saw people and businesses rise quickly, reaching great heights. But I also saw how easily they could fall. It was during these times that the way they treated others became very important.

As I moved through different jobs, I realized that being kind and respectful to others was not just the right thing to do but also very practical. People remember how you treat them, and when you need help, they are more likely to support you if you've treated them well. On the other hand, those who were arrogant often found themselves alone when they needed help.

### Learning to Adapt

In 1979, I read a book called *Future Shock* by Alvin Toffler. At the time, I didn't fully realize its importance and read it more like a novel. But there was one part that stuck with me, and it's something I've thought about ever since. The idea was simple: "The illiterate of the 21st century will not be those who cannot read or write, but those who cannot learn, unlearn, and re-learn."

Over the years, this thought has proved to be more and more relevant, especially as the world has changed so quickly in recent decades. We live in an age where technology is advancing rapidly, and it's easy to fall behind if you're not willing to keep learning. I've seen many people struggle because they hold on too tightly to what they already know. They find it hard to let go of old ways of doing things, and this can prevent them from moving forward.

I've learned that being open to new ideas and willing to change your way of thinking is essential. It's not enough to rely on what you already know. You must be ready to adapt, to let go of what doesn't work anymore, and to keep learning new things.

## My MBA Days

In 1983, I started my MBA classes. This was the decade when MBAs were considered as the "Masters" of everything to do with business and finance. An MBA degree was accompanied by big egos and a "we know it all, so we can fix it" attitude. There was a sense of confidence that sometimes turned into overconfidence.

On the first day of my MBA class, we had a course on Human Behavior and Organization (HBO). The professor, who had a very practical approach, began by cautioning us against letting the MBA degree inflate our egos. He shared a simple but powerful message: "Don't think that just because you have an MBA, you know everything. There have been times when MBAs went into a company and turned it around, only to realize later that the company was already facing in the right direction."

This advice stayed with me. It taught me to be humble and to understand that just because you have knowledge doesn't mean you always know what's best. Throughout my career, especially in roles where I was involved in transforming institutions, I kept this lesson in mind. Sometimes, the best approach is to recognize what is already working well and support it, rather than making changes just for the sake of it.

### *The Balance of Power and Responsibility*

We've all heard that with "Great Knowledge" comes "Great Power." Education gives us the tools to use our skills and make a positive difference in society. But there's another important lesson: "With Great Power comes Great Responsibility." This idea, made famous by Spider-Man, is something that is true in every part of life.

When power is used carelessly, it can lead to serious problems, whether in business, finance, or other areas of society. Today, with the advancements in technology and AI, we have more power than ever to solve problems. But this also means there's a greater risk of using that power in ways that can cause harm.

We see this happening in how financial services are offered, how data is used, and how technology is sometimes turned towards harmful purposes instead of helpful ones. These are just a few examples of what can happen when power is not handled with care.

I've realized that it's not just about having power or knowledge— it's about how we use them. The choices we make can either help or hurt. The decisions we take, especially when we have the power to make a big impact, shape not only our success but also the lives of those around us.

### *Taking Charge of Your Career*

One of the biggest lessons I've learned in my career is that **you are the only one responsible for your own path**. Whether your bosses are supportive or difficult, it's up to you to make sure you're doing the right thing. It's about using the opportunities your company gives you to do what's best for everyone involved and helps in meeting your career goals.

I believe we all have moments when something we read, hear, or see sticks with us, leaving a lasting impression in our minds. These small pieces of knowledge can play a big role in shaping our values and how others see us in society. The way we use and apply this information influences not just our actions but also how those around us perceive us.

Throughout my life, I have made it a point to share my experiences and learnings with the people I come across in both my personal and professional life. I am especially fond of ensuring that our youth get the right messages to learn from the good and bad of our generation's experiences. For example, I shared the following messages with a group of young entrepreneurs at a conference in Bahrain in 2019:

***Key Messages delivered to Young Entrepreneurs and Innovators at a conference in Bahrain (2019)***

- The opportunities to build an inclusive future better than the past are within reach, given the more powerful tools we now have in the form of technology. Therefore, innovate for sustainability and ease the lives of 85%+ of the global population who are struggling to make ends meet. Identify the pain points and innovate to redress them.

- Always remember that the kind of future you build as an entrepreneur depends on how responsible you are in building it. Most important of all, innovate with responsibility and empathy.

- Regulations follow innovation; so, entrepreneurs and innovators must make sure to leave a track record of responsible behavior. Otherwise, regulations that follow may stifle innovation.

- While data is fast becoming a commodity and will be used in all innovations and entrepreneurship endeavors that leverage technology, make sure that its collection, structuring, and use are undertaken responsibly.

- Responsible innovation includes ensuring that any ML being undertaken, or algorithms being developed are not reflecting biases of persons/institutions developing them.

- As entrepreneurs and innovators, you may be constrained by legacy ecosystems made for legacy institutions; so be part of the dialogue to change them.

- Make sure to leverage each other for strength; ensure you have a platform to interact with regulators/other stakeholders so that the regulatory, legislative, and other eco-systems to be put in place are aligned with what your innovation wants to achieve.

- Challenge the legacy education systems and influence and demand changes so that they match your expectations of learning (and even unlearning and relearning).

- Learn from experienced legacy professionals; perhaps more of what not to do.

During my time at IFC, I saw it as a place that allowed me to provide financial and advisory services in a way that mattered. This wasn't always easy because of challenges like bureaucracy, internal competition, and unclear goals. But being part of a respected institution like IFC made a difference. It helped my voice be heard and my efforts make an impact.

A strong company can open doors and let you be part of important decisions. But this only works if you know how to make the most of what the company offers. One thing I regret about the WBG is that, even though it's a powerful institution, the way it's run often weakens the impact it could have on the developing world.

## "Mentoring: A Two-Way Street"

I have always enjoyed mentoring young people for their professional development and helping them become good human beings. From advising high school students on career choices to guiding graduate students at my alma mater and other universities and supporting colleagues and teammates at the companies I've worked for; I have always found it fulfilling to share my experiences and knowledge. I've also had the privilege of being part of formal mentoring programs at IFC and the Asian Institute of Management.

*Here are some testimonials from people who either reported to me or were part of my mentorship network:*

*"Very grateful to Kaiser, who has been not only my direct supervisor but, over the years we worked alongside, turned into a trusted senior friend and mentor. He skillfully helped me navigate through the ups and downs of growing professionally in a multicultural corporate environment. He also gave me valuable lessons in building long-lasting relationships, not only within the organization but with our clients' companies. Big thank you, dear friend and mentor."*

**— Ulugbek Tilyayev**
***Bank Advisory Services,***
***International Finance Corporation***

*"Kaiser Sir's mentorship during my time at business school was pivotal in shaping my career. His insightful career coaching and entrepreneurial guidance gave me the confidence to take bold steps and make informed decisions."*

**— Vikram Dhar, EMBA 2023**
***Asian Institute of Management***

*"Kaiser Naseem's mentorship and guidance during the early years of our establishing Alif Group Tajikistan were instrumental in our success today. This guidance, strategic advice and mentorship continues to this day. I very much value and appreciate the continued support provided by Kaiser".*

**— Abdullo Kurbanov**
***Co-Founder Alif Group***

*"I worked in Kaiser's team when he was heading Corporate Governance Advisory. He has been a great mentor to me. His key strength as a mentor has been his belief in delegating tasks to his team members. That helped foster both a sense of ownership of the team's goals and accountability for individual outcomes. As a result, his delegation approach helped his team members grow professionally and become leaders in their respective areas of responsibility."*

**— Mohsin Choudhary**
***Corporate Governance Advisory Services,***
***International Finance Corporation***

For me, a good leader is one who shares his or her knowledge, work ethic, and habits with the aim of helping others grow into better professionals and individuals. But mentoring isn't a one-way street. I've learned a great deal from the people I've mentored, with most of this learning coming from the feedback they have given me, both formally and informally.

At IFC, I often told my colleagues that the true measure of my success as a manager would be if, someday, they ended up being my boss. Many of them went on to lead teams as large, if not larger, than mine, which remains one of my proudest achievements.

# Chapter 12

# A Life of Purpose

Looking back, I feel a great sense of pride and satisfaction in having chosen a career that focused on improving people's lives through economic development. The journey wasn't always easy but knowing that my work made a real difference is something I hold close to my heart.

On the global stage, it's unfortunate that rivalry and blame continue to dominate international relations and politics. The constant finger-pointing between countries like the USA, China, and Russia does little to solve the problems we face. In recent years, we've seen so much destruction and chaos. Some of it has been due to natural disasters, but much of it is the result of human actions. Wars have taken millions of lives and disrupted even more livelihoods.

It's sad to see that many world leaders seem to lack the vision and leadership needed to improve things. Instead of working toward a better future, many are stuck in conflicts that only make matters worse.

As I conclude this book, the 79th session of the United Nations General Assembly (UNGA79) is taking place in New York, amidst a chaotic world embroiled in conflicts, economic inequality and the imminent threat of climate change. As we know, this session is attended by world leaders, including presidents, prime ministers and diplomats. In his opening remarks, the UN Secretary General, Antonio Guterres warned "Our world is on a powder keg" he said. "We can't go on like this". He then asked a rhetorical question: "Have we forgotten the UN mission?" In my opinion, although born out of a desire for peace in 1945, the institution has long been toothless.

Yes, the world has made progress, reducing poverty from around 40% in the 1990s to about 18% today. But this progress is not evenly spread. In many countries, poverty levels have actually risen. While people continue to face hardships in 2024, governments seem more interested in playing politics than in genuinely improving the lives of their citizens. This focus on politics leaves many people uncertain about their future.

What the world really needs now is a level of collaboration, information sharing, and funding like never before to truly make a difference. We saw a glimpse of this during the COVID-19 pandemic in 2020, where there was a spirit of cooperation, but sadly, it faded away soon after. The key takeaway is clear: when there's a genuine willingness to work together for the common good, the world can achieve remarkable things.

If we truly lived up to even half of the promises and pledges, we make, using words like honesty, ethics, justice, good governance, inclusivity, diversity, and sustainability, the world would be much closer to becoming the "heaven on earth" we aimed for by 2030 through the 17 SDGs. Unfortunately, achieving these goals by then now seems very unlikely. It's not just up to governments; each of us needs to take conscious, informed, and responsible actions. And when I say each of us, I mean everyone, not just half the population. We need to bring women fully into the economic development equation by enabling them, empowering them, and giving them access to all resources. They need to be equal partners in these efforts. This is not happening fast enough. Unless we have 100% effort, we will never have 100% impact.

The 2020s have brought the world into the digital era, with many people finding themselves adjusting to this new reality, whether they were ready or not. With the increased use of technology, there's also been a rise in cyber-crimes, largely due to the irresponsible and unethical use of digital tools, which still causes concern for many. There are still several regulatory and operational challenges that need to be addressed, especially in developing markets and for women, who often face additional barriers to accessing and benefiting from technology.

Businesses have made efforts to accept digitalization, but this shift has also revealed some weaknesses. One key issue is how data is managed and used. Many companies have found that their data is often stored in separate systems, making it difficult to access and use effectively. Digitalizing businesses is really about how data is managed. There's still a lot of work to be done in this area. On the other side, consumers have become more aware of the need to be careful with their data. Cybersecurity remains a significant risk for all types of businesses.

It's clear that despite all the awareness and advocacy around issues like responsible behavior, sustainable development, and good governance, we still see irresponsible actions, even from global institutions that should be setting an example. International financial institutions have a big role to play in the economic development of countries and could drive real change alongside other global organizations. But for this to happen, these institutions need to truly commit to their purpose. They should not only talk about responsible finance, good governance, climate change, and sustainable development but actually lead by example. Just talking about these issues hasn't made a big difference so far, and it won't in the future either.

We've been pushing for the world to focus on getting rid of harmful practices like child labor, poor environmental practices, and irresponsible finance. While these issues are now on the radar and people are more aware of them, there's still a gap between what's being said and what's being done.

Hope keeps us moving forward, pushing us to work toward a more inclusive world. It's with this hope that we must continue to strive for a better future. The future will be shaped by our actions and the choices we make today.

Thankfully, we now have the tools to ensure that the future can be brighter than the past. One of the most powerful tools at our disposal is technology. But this tool needs to be used responsibly and for meaningful purposes, like re-educating and retraining workers who are anxious about how technology will affect their jobs. More and more people are expressing concerns about globalization and technology. They feel that the benefits have so far only reached a small fraction of the world's population, leaving many, especially the middle class, with stagnant or declining incomes and few opportunities. This is a worrying trend because if large groups of people begin to see technology and globalization as threats rather than opportunities, they may push for changes that could set economies back.

We continue to see global financial institutions investing large sums of money into countries where the results don't match the funds provided. These institutions are starting to face challenges and embarrassments in places like Argentina, Pakistan, Egypt, and several other countries.

Still, I believe that there are many people—men, women, and even children—who are tirelessly working to improve life on our planet and beyond. Thanks to the efforts of these individuals, both big and small, we continue to make progress and look toward the future with hope. Today, we see more private sector players supporting the green economy and using their influence to implement important changes. More companies are striving to follow good governance and social standards to connect with their customers and stay relevant. Social media has also become a powerful tool, giving people a platform to voice their concerns and demand the changes that so many are fighting for.

George Bernard Shaw once said, *"Life is no brief candle for me. It is a sort of splendid torch, which I must hold for the moment, and I want to make it burn as brightly as possible before handing it on to future generations."* If we were to pass this torch to today's youth, it wouldn't shine as brightly as it should. Instead of a clear and guiding light, it seems more like a flicker struggling to break through the smog, fog, and illusions that cloud our present. The bright future that the baby-boomer generation should have passed down to the next generation is now overshadowed by the challenges we've created or ignored.

We may have missed our chance to make the necessary changes, as Christine Lagarde, the former head of the IMF, once warned when she said, "Make reforms while the sun shines on the world economy." These words, though well-intended, now seem hollow, especially if that sunshine only reached 1% of the world's population.

The true purpose of life is to live with purpose. It's time for us to commit to making the coming years ones of true purposefulness, filled with tolerance, empathy, and a willingness to learn, unlearn and relearn. We need to ensure we have the right infrastructure and mindset to get back on track with the Sustainable Development Goals (SDGs) we set for ourselves. Let's use the platforms available to us to spread this message far and wide. More importantly, let's turn our words into actions and work together to create a brighter future for all.

## A Life of Learning, Unlearning, and Relearning

With all the years behind me, witnessing so much change and so many events, I've remained constant in my journey of learning, unlearning, and relearning. Throughout this long and winding path, I've met people from all walks of life—each encounter adding a new layer to my understanding of the world. Some journeys were filled with joy, others with challenges, but they all contributed to who I am today.

The one thing that has always stayed with me, something that I hold dear, is the work I did as a development banker. It was the longest journey of my life, and what made it truly rewarding was knowing that the work I was doing was making a difference. The best part about being a development banker wasn't just the projects or the numbers; it was knowing that I was part of something much bigger—something that was helping to shape the future and improve lives.

In many ways, the developments I worked on were not just for the economies or the communities; they were for me as a person too. This journey has taught me kindness, patience, empathy, and a deep sense of contentment. It has made me appreciate the small things, the connections with people, and the impact that thoughtful actions can have. The work wasn't always easy. There were many sacrifices along the way—both personally and professionally. But when I look back, none of it feels like a hardship. Instead, it feels like the necessary steps that brought me to where I am today.

The true purpose of life is to live with purpose. Over the years, I've come to understand that this is the guiding principle that should shape our actions. It's time for all of us to commit to living with purpose, to making the coming years ones filled with meaning. We need to be driven by tolerance, empathy, and an openness to learn, unlearn, and relearn. These are the qualities that will help us grow and adapt in a world that's constantly changing.

It's also essential that we focus on building the right infrastructure and mindset to achieve the Sustainable Development Goals (SDGs) we've set for ourselves. These goals are not just targets; they are a blueprint for a better world. But for them to become a reality, we need to turn our words into actions. We need to use every platform available to us to spread this message and encourage others to do the same.

I realised that the work I did wasn't just about meeting targets or fulfilling job requirements. It was about making a lasting impact. It was about contributing to something greater than myself. And it was about leaving the world a little better than I found it.

I've learned that life is not just about personal success or achievements. It's about purpose, about making a difference in the lives of others. As I close this book, I do so with a sense of fulfillment and hope that the torch I've carried will be passed on to others who will continue this work with the same passion and dedication.

*I believe that the true measure of a life well-lived is not in the titles we hold or the wealth we accumulate, but in the positive changes we bring to the world around us. That, for me, is the essence of living a life of purpose.*

# The Journey Continues

As fate would have it, the last leg of my more than a quarter of a century career with IFC brought me back to Moscow. In mid-2017 I was posted to IFC's Eastern Europe and Central Asia Region with Moscow as the regional office. So, I relocated to a city in which I had spent a large part of my youth.

Of course, Moscow is a city I know very well. I used to tell people that I could find my way around Moscow blindfolded. But in all these years, it has changed a lot. For one, it is no longer the capital of the USSR but now the capital of Russia. It retains its beauty and splendor as a city, even more so.

When I lived in Moscow during the 1970s it was hard to imagine that the USSR would someday fall apart. While the system had several issues, like any other system, it was working well. The country had 100% employment and, by and large, people were satisfied and happy. There were the usual lot who, like in any other nation, were critical of the way the country was being run. But that was not a huge majority.

When we used to discuss the communist system among ourselves, or with our local friends, there was always one issue

I emphasized upon. That was the lack of freedom to travel outside the USSR. Owing to this unnecessary restriction on travel, the people would imagine all sorts of things about the western countries, based on propaganda and hearsay. They would think that all the citizens of those countries lived a life of luxury and had lots of money to spend. Had they been allowed to travel abroad and visit cities like New York, Los Angels, London, Paris, and others, they would have realized that these countries had issues of their own, such as unemployment, poverty, homelessness, very little social protection, and so on. The citizens of those countries had to struggle hard to make a living. Perhaps, they would have then valued their system more, despite all its drawbacks. Today, in Russia face similar issues, and one can see the big divide between the rich and the poor, the haves and the have-nots. The citizens of Russia are still trying to come to grips with this reality, even after more than 30 years.

In any case, this is now history, and the USSR collapsed in 1991 with each of its 15 republics declaring themselves as independent countries.

Back in Moscow, I really enjoyed meeting old friends and visiting old haunts, especially my alma mater. I got the sense that there was both a feeling of happiness and nostalgia in the air. The youth had adapted to the new way of life, whereas some old-timers were still struggling to find their place. While the people have moved on, politics still seems to be standing still. The relationship between the USA and Russia, which had become rather cordial in the 1990s, is again at its lowest ebb. Each is again vying for world domination. All I can say is that the United States of America lost a great opportunity to step up and help build and lead a much better and a more peaceful world. It could have done this in the 1990s when it was globally recognized as the only superpower. But as the Pulitzer Prize-winning journalist Chris Hedges says in his article Chronicle of War Foretold, "How naive we were. And here we are. On the brink of another Cold War".

I had just been a couple of months in my new role in Moscow when sanctions were imposed on Russia by the USA and its allies. The west blamed Russia for interfering in the 2016 US elections and meddling in the affairs of Ukraine. Soon after, we received instructions from the IFC head office telling us not to solicit any additional projects in the country. We were only allowed to complete the ongoing ones. This was indeed sad, as the World Bank Group should be apolitical and not toe the line of any one country. After all, Russia is also a member country of the WBG and deserves to avail its assistance to meet its economic development objectives.

At IFC, most of our focus was on assisting well-established companies. These companies had better chances of success and creating an impact and thus provided a good story for IFC. The idea was that the second-tier companies would follow and replicate that success. But this rarely happened. Despite the success of larger companies, the second-tier ones still struggled to grow on their own.

This made me start questioning how development assistance was being delivered and whether it was really reaching those who needed it the most.

Whenever I visited a country, these second-tier companies would often approach me with the same question: Why does IFC only focus on larger, well-established companies that already have access to financial and technical support? It was the second tier and less robust businesses that needed help to grow and contribute to economic development.

This question always stayed with me. I saw firsthand how these smaller second-tier companies were struggling. They had potential – the potential to innovate, create jobs, and contribute to the economy. But they lacked the resources, guidance, and support to take the next step.

Over the years, I kept thinking about this. I decided that once I retired from IFC, I wanted to play a role in helping these types of businesses grow, especially in developing countries where they needed it most. Providing support to such companies could make a real and meaningful difference.

The opportunity to pursue this passion came sooner than I expected, through the IFC Voluntary Separation Scheme (VSS). It felt like the right time for me to step into this new phase of helping smaller businesses navigate the complex economic challenges they face, both locally and globally.

In December 2019, I decided to take early retirement from IFC and opted for the Voluntary Separation Scheme (VSS). I left IFC on January 01, 2020.

Over the years, I have learned that real change often comes from those sitting at the highest levels of decision-making – the boards of directors (BOD). These are the people with the authority to set strategic direction and provide oversight. I knew that if I wanted to make a difference, I needed to be involved at that level.

After leaving IFC in early 2020, I actively sought opportunities to work with companies in developing markets, particularly by joining their BOD. My goal was simple: to help these companies build capacity, adopt sustainable practices, and empower them to succeed in a constantly evolving world. I wanted to use my years of experience to help these businesses grow.

In mid-2020, I got my first chance. I was invited to join the BOD of one of Uzbekistan's state-owned banks. The goal was to help the bank transform into a more commercially driven institution, attract private investors, and eventually privatize it. This was all part of the Government of Uzbekistan's (GOU) larger plan to reform the banking sector and modernize the country's economy.

Over the next two years, I took on roles at more than six different boards of directors (BODs). In line with good corporate governance practices, it's generally advised that one shouldn't be on more than four or five boards, as it becomes harder to dedicate enough time and attention to each one. Quality input, especially during board meetings, is crucial. I was mindful of this and decided to choose a variety of companies, each with different needs and challenges.

I ended up sitting on the boards of various types of companies. There was this bank in Uzbekistan, a microfinance institution in Kyrgyzstan, and a tech startup in Dubai that focused on the emerging metaverse space. In addition to these, I also joined the BOD of another microfinance institution in Poland, a corporate governance institute in Pakistan, a Fintech startup, and a non-profit organization in San Francisco. This last one works to give a voice to small shareholders and engages in other advocacy activities, mainly focused on climate governance.

The skills set I bring to a Board of Directors includes areas like Digital Transformation, Strategy Formulation, MSME Banking, Sustainable Development, Climate Risk, and Corporate Governance. As I started serving on these boards, I quickly saw the enormous potential within these smaller institutions I was involved with. These companies, often with limited resources, were filled with individuals who were ready to take risks, think differently, and challenge traditional ways of doing things.

Being surrounded by such motivated individuals allowed us to explore new opportunities, adjust strategies, and find solutions to the challenges of our time—whether it was technology, sustainable development, or good governance. It wasn't just about business growth; it was about making a meaningful difference for those who had the courage to pursue their ambitions despite the odds.

Apart from my board roles, I also took up public speaking at various conferences, workshops, and events. I now share the experiences and lessons I had gathered throughout my career, especially focusing on topics that are gaining importance globally like digitalisation, climate change, corporate governance, entrepreneurship, and MSME development. I aim to reach a broader audience, particularly the younger generation, and provide them with insights that could help shape their future decisions.

As I reflect on this new chapter of my life, I feel grateful for all the experiences that have brought me here. Leaving IFC was not the end of my journey; it was the start of something new. It gave me the chance to work on something that means a lot to me.

I began this new phase with a clear purpose: to help the smaller, second-tier companies in emerging markets. These businesses often have big dreams but lack the resources and support to achieve them. I wanted to help close the gap between their ambition and the opportunities they needed. By doing this, I hoped to help these companies grow and make a positive difference in their communities.

# About the Author

*Dr. Kaiser Naseem, a Canadian citizen of Pakistani origin is an international development banker with over 40 years of experience in banking and development finance, including 26 years with the IFC/World Bank Group. He has helped in developing financial institutions and innovative business models in challenging environments. Dr. Naseem's expertise spans project finance, digital transformation, strategy formulation, MSME banking, sustainable development, ESG/ Climate Risk, and corporate governance. He serves on several Boards of Directors globally, providing strategic guidance and mentoring to senior management and business owners.*

*Recognized as a global leader in development finance, Dr. Naseem was awarded an Honorary Doctorate in Development Finance and Economics in 2022. He was named one of the Top 50 Fintech Influencers in the Middle East in 2018 and a Top 100 Global Fintech Influencer for SDGs in 2019.*

*Throughout his career, Dr. Kaiser Naseem has worked across the Middle East, North Africa, Eastern and Southern Europe, Central Asia, and North America.*

# Gallery

With my mother and brothers, Athar Naseem and Fouad Naseem
(Karachi 2003)

With my parents and brother Athar (Washington DC circa 1960)

My brother Athar and I in Washington DC (circa 1961)

My brother and I with Santa Claus in Washington DC (circa 1961)

When starting my professional career
(Karachi 1979)

With my sons Hammad and Hisham (Islamabad 1995)

With my daughter Sahar and sons Hammad and Hisham
(Washington DC 1996)

With my wife Saira in New Delhi (2002)

Being awarded by Prime Minister of Pakistan for my work in
SME sector (2006)

Completing the Board Certification Program (Karachi 2007)

Supporting an education NGO in Indonesia (2024)

The Indonesian NGO's classroom

With my daughters Sahar and Anusheh in Orlando (2013)

At the famous Dr. Zhivago restaurant in Moscow with my wife (2018)

The Moscow Metro (2018)

The Bolshoi Theatre in Moscow (2018)

Outside the Bolshoi Theatre in Moscow (2018)

Another Moscow underground station (2018)

Received award for my work in Development Finance (Singapore 2019)

At an Entrepreneurs' Conference in Bahrain (2019)

At Kafe Tchaikovsky, Moscow (2019)

With my wife Saira at the Red Square, Moscow (2019)

In front of my Alma Mater (MISIS) in Moscow (2019)

At the World Economic Forum in Davos with my sons (2020)

Covid times together with my wife (Dubai 2020)

With my wife Saira and her parents in Dubai (2021)

Awarded a PhD in Development Finance (2021)

With my wife, daughter, sons and grandchildren (Dubai 2021)

At dinner with the family - Dubai (2021)

Keynote speech at Emirates Centre for Strategic Studies and Research
(Abu Dhabi 2021)

With my family: Saira, Sahar, Hammad, Hisham and Anusheh (2022)

With my wife in Samarkand (2022)

Saira and I at our home in Dubai (2023)

With the board of Xalq Bank Uzbekistan (2022)

At a conference in Dubai (2022)

With Saira in Tashkent (2022)

With Saira at the Samarkand Economic Forum, Uzbekistan (2022)

At the Uzbekistan Economic Forum in Samarkand (2022)

With my Xalq Bank BOD colleagues in Samarkand (2022)

Relaxing at Lake Como, Italy (2023)

With my wife Saira and daughter Anusheh in Milano, Italy (2023)

With my wife Saira (2023)

Outside our home in Dubai (2023)

Outside our home with Saira and Anusheh (2024)

With my wife Saira and daughter Anusheh (Dubai 2024)

Relaxing with my wife at Lake Como, Italy (2023)

At the Museum of the Future in Dubai with my daughter's family (2024)